"When I began working with Lisa, I needed to really strengthen my resume and make my experience stand out. I wasn't sure where to start. Lisa's approach was easy to follow and her ___ only taught me how to u___ ___ to evaluate my background ___ ___ I would be prepared for any q___ during job interviews. These are ___ been able to use during my job ___

"During interviews, I'm not always effective at communicating stories that demonstrate what I've achieved throughout my career. I often get nervous and forget what to say. Lisa knew exactly what I needed to do in order to get over nerves and showcase my skills – create a portfolio of work examples in a 3-ring binder to bring to job interviews. I can now easily flip to one of my examples and use it to explain the situation, what I did, and the results I achieved. With Lisa's guidance, I'm now much more confident going into interviews."
– Tricia B.

"After many years working in political consulting and fundraising, I decided I wanted to change careers. The problem? I wasn't sure how or if my background would translate into the new career I wanted. Using Lisa's approach of analyzing job postings against my skills and experience, I was able to update my resume to showcase the attributes and accomplishments that were most applicable. The result? I landed a great job in the industry I wanted!" – Sarah R.

"After almost 20 years in the retail industry, I needed a career change. Lisa's step-by-step process for switching industries gave me confidence in my ability to move into another career. She helped me realize the importance of taking the time to step back and strategically look at my options, opportunities, and direction and then she helped me prioritize my actions. Lisa also suggested different strategies for uncovering my next career move that I would have never considered, like job shadowing. It isn't just for kids – it works well for anyone trying to decide on several different types of jobs. I'm now happily working in a new career that I love." – Kristi H.

REAL PEOPLE, REAL EXPERIENCES

"Previously my career choices haven't always been good decisions. I have often accepted positions based on the job being the first thing that comes along or on compensation. These decisions have proven not to be a good fit for me. Lisa's job search process helped me realize that I needed to look at the interview process from a different angle – that they are an opportunity for me to uncover whether the job, the manager, and the company are actually a good fit for me. Lisa also taught me the right questions to ask during the interviews to obtain the information I needed to make better job decisions. An additional bonus to this process is now I'm more confident and comfortable in job interview situations because I'm prepared. " – Kim F.

"Lisa's techniques for job seekers really work, especially her methods to professionally close an interview from the candidate's perspective. Before, I used to leave interviews wondering how I'd done or if I'd hear back. Then Lisa taught me a questioning process so I could leave interviews knowing what the hiring manager thought about my fit for the position, the next steps in the hiring process, and when he or she would be making their hiring decision. The best part? I followed Lisa's process and received a job offer after my very next interview. Truly amazing!" – Amanda S.

"I spent 15 years working for one company, then the economy crashed and the entire department was let go due to downsizing. While it would normally be terrifying to look for a job after all those years of steady employment, Lisa's thoughtful job seeking techniques made the process easy and as stress free as possible. My confidence grew as I completed each of Lisa's recommended steps and then began receiving requests for job interviews. Throughout my career, I've used several coaches and Lisa Quast is the best I've ever met. Her unique background and experience gives her an edge over other career coaches. Lisa knows what it takes for a woman to make it to the executive level at a Fortune 500 company in male-dominated industries (because she's done it herself), she's a successful entrepreneur, and she's been a business consultant, organizational trainer, and executive coach for companies all over the world. I trust her techniques because I've used them – and they all work! " – Linda J.

SECRETS
of a
HIRING MANAGER
turned
CAREER COACH

A FOOLPROOF GUIDE
TO GETTING THE
JOB YOU WANT.
EVERY TIME.

LISA QUAST

SECRETS OF A HIRING MANAGER TURNED CAREER COACH: A *Foolproof Guide To Getting The Job You Want. Every Time.*

LISA QUAST

Editor: Shauna Nuckles, Revolution PR
Cover design and book layout: Aaron Hilst Design
Publisher: Career Woman, Inc.

Career Woman Inc.
www.careerwomaninc.com

Revolution PR
www.revolutionpr.com

Aaron Hilst
www.aaronhilst.com

ISBN: 978-1-936048-13-7

Library Of Congress Control Number: 2014915099

Career Woman, Inc., Issaquah, Washington

DEDICATION

This book is dedicated to all women around the world. You are smart, beautiful, and you each have the potential to achieve your dreams and your life's purpose. Like butterflies, you hold deep within yourself the energy to transform into the person you want to be. In reading this book, my hope is that you will discover your wings and soar to great heights – living your life and your career in a way that benefits all humankind.

TABLE OF CONTENTS

PART 5 – SCORE AN INTERVIEW

PART 6 – PREP FOR INTERVIEW SUCCESS

PART 7 – ACE THE INTERVIEW

PART 8 – AFTER THE INTERVIEW

INTRODUCTION

Over the last few years I've seen and heard a lot of the crazy things people have done to get a job. Desperate job seekers have done everything from auctioning themselves off on eBay to purchasing ads boasting their work skills to singing their resume in a YouTube video. I've even heard of someone who sent the hiring manager their name and contact information in frosting on top of a gigantic cookie.

While these are creative ideas, sending hiring managers your resume in a pop-up box that explodes glittering stars when opened won't get you hired if you haven't mastered the job seeking basics.

What this book IS: If you're looking for everything you need to know to obtain a job (or change careers) and want to learn the job seeking basics in an easy-to-follow, step-by-step manner that makes sense… then this book is for you. Keep reading.

What this book IS NOT: If you're looking for crazy ways to catch the attention of a hiring manager, such as paying to have an airplane pilot fly a "Hire Me" banner over the company or using a singing telegram service to deliver your resume to an unsuspecting hiring manager… then this book is not for you. Go ahead and put it down right now or give it to a friend.

Who this book is FOR: While both women and men can apply the techniques in this book, I have purposely written it to help women. Almost all of the examples and stories included are from real women (names changed) I've coached over the last twenty years. My passion in life has been and continues to be to help women achieve their career dreams and fulfill their purpose in life.

Recommended process: To obtain the most benefit from this book, I recommend you find a quiet location to relax and enjoy reading it cover-to-cover in a few sittings. Then, go back to each chapter and work through the job seeking exercises over a period of several weeks or months. This approach will provide you with a thorough understanding of the work you'll need to complete throughout the job search process.

Why I'm the author of this book: When it comes to the job search process, I've been involved in every aspect and from every angle. I've been a job seeker myself, stumbling through the process and trying to figure out what to do. I've sat on the other side of the table as a hiring manager, interviewing thousands of candidates for jobs at large, global corporations and trying to find those who best fit the open positions. I've trained recruiters, HR personnel, and other hiring managers on the techniques to find and hire the right people. And, I've coached countless clients through the job search process with a 100% success rate.

Early in my career I defined my aspirations – to either make it to the executive level of a Fortune 500 company or own my own business. I knew that to achieve either of these goals I'd have to learn as much as possible about every aspect of business, so I made it my mission to work in almost every area of a company. I have experience in: sales; service; marketing; communications; product management; operations; project management and process improvement; business development; strategic planning; mergers, acquisitions, and alliances; and talent/organizational development. Throughout my corporate career, I also worked closely with finance, human resources, quality and regulatory, legal, and IT personnel.

This extensive background (combined with three college degrees, two certifications, and ongoing educational pursuits), has given me the unique ability to hire people and coach clients in almost every department within a company. And what I've learned throughout my career and from my time coaching others is that finding a job (or changing careers) takes a lot of thought and preparation. *It isn't as simple as merely posting your resume on a few electronic job board sites. To find a position that is a good fit requires a thoughtful, strategic approach.*

The best way to ensure a good job fit is by following the process I explain in this book, which includes everything from sitting down and determining the kind of job you want, defining your career goals, conducting research and personal analysis, developing your documents and your personal brand, preparing for interviews and following up afterwards. Take a look at the *Table of Contents* and you'll see what I mean… obtaining your dream job requires following a process that is built on a foundation of job seeking basics.

Bottom Line: Before you attempt any new or trendy job seeking tactics, first ensure you have the basics covered. The basics are the "must-haves" whereas creative maneuvers should come only after the fundamentals are well executed (if at all).

So grab a cup of coffee (or tea) and let's get started.

~ Your Career Coach, Lisa

FIND YOUR PASSION

FIND YOUR PASSION

GIVE YOURSELF A PERSONAL "TIME OUT"

Finding a job you love isn't easy. For many, life goes by quickly and before you know it, you find yourself stuck in a not-so-great job, working for a boss you don't like, wondering how you got there. How do you find a career you're passionate about? First, take a personal "time out" from the chaos of life and the workplace for some reflection.

Shortly after graduating from college, I struggled to figure out what I wanted to do for my long-term career. At the time, I was working at a job I disliked for an insecure manager who seemed jealous of all her employees. I was also working long hours, which made my attitude, personal life, and health suffer.

One evening, my sister took me out to dinner and handed me a wrapped box with a bow on top. *"What's this?"* I asked.

"Just a little something I saw, and I thought of you," she said. When I unwrapped the gift I found a picture in a frame with the caption, 'Find your passion.'

I thanked my sister and then sighed. *"But that's exactly my problem. I can't seem to figure out my passion at work."*

"Maybe you're trying too hard," she replied. *"Sometimes you just have to take a step back, relax, and try to see the big picture. Stop worrying about finding another job and start thinking about what makes you happy and uncovering the things you're great at doing."*

My sister had a good point. It is easy to get so caught up in the everyday details of work that eventually misery becomes your focus. When that happens, it's our first instinct to start looking for a new job. But jumping from one ill-fitting job to the next could cause even more heartache (and headache).

I listened to my sister's advice and took a personal "time out." The next weekend I went for a relaxing walk on the beach (I was living in California at the time) and thought about my life. Then I sat in the sand, pulled out a notepad and pen, and began answering these questions:

- What makes me happy?
- What adjectives would people who know me use to describe me?
- What are my core values in life?
- What is my definition of success?
- What am I good at accomplishing at work?
- What tasks do I dislike at work?
- What do I want to be known for?

Completing this exercise confirmed what I had been feeling – I was in the wrong job. I realized there were certain jobs I just wasn't meant to do. They did not fit with what I was really good at, what I liked doing, or what I wanted to accomplish in my career.

Realizing this, these answers motivated me to take the next step of trying to clarify the type of job that would better fit my skills, values, and passions in life. A week later (after another walk on the beach), I wrote down answers to my next set of questions:

- What is the description of my perfect job?
- With what kind of people would I like to be working?
- How should my work benefit me?
- How should my work benefit other people?
- How should my work make me feel?

Answering these questions helped me begin to explore other job options. That exploration led to a career I loved in marketing and then into other areas of business, such as strategic planning. For me, finding my career passion was as much about learning to understand myself as it was about finding a job that was a better fit. Once I found a job I loved, great things began happening in my career.

Sometimes, searching for a job or trying to find a different job can be so frustrating and stressful that it becomes overwhelming. It is important to recognize when you are feeling overwhelmed, so you can give yourself a personal "time out." Give yourself permission to take a break for a week or two from conducting any kind of job search or research. Then, follow these three steps to help you to move forward.

First, find 10 minutes each day to meditate. If you've never done this don't worry – it's actually pretty easy. Find a quiet place to sit or lie down. Be still. Clear your mind of everything, and try to relax. Picture yourself in a peaceful place, and, as if you are standing in a shower, envision a bright white, cleansing light pouring over your entire body and clearing out all your fears, stress, and anxiety. Simply be still, be quiet, and allow this light to continue pouring over you.

After you feel yourself relaxing, ask the Universe to point you in the best direction for your next job or career. Don't be shy – ask for blatant signs of the direction you should pursue. Then, as you go about your normal daily routines, try to keep a watchful eye for what you might see. You may be surprised at the funny ways the Universe will give you signs, so be prepared to laugh when you see some of them.

I did this process in reverse once, and received a pretty amusing response. At the time, I was feeling frustrated in my job so while I meditated, I asked the Universe to give me clear signs to show me if I should stay in my current job or look for something different. The very next day the hard drive on my work laptop crashed. A few days later the telephone in my office stopped working. Then the heel on my shoe broke off while I was walking to a meeting. Finally, I ended up locked out of my office. The locksmith said the building had apparently settled a bit and that process had somehow jammed the hinges of the door, making it unable to open. That's when I realized the Universe had a pretty good sense of humor when it came to showing me signs that I should consider a different job.

Second, increase the joy in your life. Every day, do something fun. Choose things that make you happy. Read a book, see a movie, eat a dark chocolate truffle, or go for a walk. It doesn't matter what the activity is, as long as it makes you happy. Remember that feeling of excitement and happiness on the first day of summer vacation when you were a child? Those are the feelings you want to try to re-capture again as an adult. To do this, make a list of all the things that give you joy and then choose one activity each day. You'll be surprised at the positive energy you begin to feel every day when you get up in the morning.

Third, spend more time being thankful. Every night before you fall asleep, think of one thing for which you're thankful and say it in your head as you drift off to sleep. *"Today, I'm thankful for…* <insert your comment here>." Or, begin a gratitude journal, where you write down the things you are grateful for before you go to sleep each night. Most likely, you'll quickly discover many of the wonderful benefits of having an attitude of gratitude, things like: feeling happier, decreased stress, more optimistic, improved sleep, increased energy, improved productivity, increased self-awareness… and the list goes on. Being grateful, even for the challenges you face, can change your life for the better. There is an old saying, "like attracts like" – when your outlook is positive and filled with gratitude, you'll actually attract more and more positive things into your life.

Being successful at whatever job you choose means taking the time to find your passion. If you're passionate about your work, it will come across to everyone around you and help you fill your life with meaning.

Are you ready for your personal "time out"? I've placed templates for you to use at the back of this book in the Appendix (and online):

- **Personal Assessment (page 256)**
- **Future Job Assessment (page 257)**

CHAPTER 1
KEY TAKEAWAYS

To be truly happy and successful in your career, you must take the time to find your passion. If you are passionate about your work, it will come across to everyone around you and help you fill your life with meaning and purpose. To start finding your career passion, give yourself a personal "time out" by focusing on reflection and exploration.

CHAPTER 2

ASK YOURSELF WHY YOU WANT TO CHANGE JOBS

Whenever someone comes to me for coaching to obtain a different job or change careers, the first question I ask is, *"Why do you want to change jobs?"* It sounds like a simple question, right? But it's actually pretty complex, and it often leads to some soul-searching to discover why the person is unhappy in their current job and whether or not changing jobs is in their best interest.

Are you considering a different job? Before you jump into the job seeker process, take the time to consider *why* you want to change jobs. Grab a cup of coffee, sit down, relax, and write out your list of reasons. For example, maybe you want a new job because you feel your manager isn't supportive of your career development, or you're bored and want to do something more challenging. You might be having difficulty with a coworker who keeps taking credit for your work or ideas, or you're just plain tired of your manager's verbally abusive behavior. Whatever your reasons, write them down.

Now, read through your list of reasons for wanting to leave your job and see if you can put each reason into one of these three categories:

1) Issues within my **manager's** ability to control.

2) Issues within **my** ability to control.

3) Issues **outside** of my manager's and my ability to control.

Really think deeply about the underlying cause of each issue. If you feel like your manager isn't supportive of your career development, you might at first put this into the "Issues within my manager's ability to control" and then think to yourself, *"Yeah, right. Like he/she even cares one way or another about my career."* But what if you looked at the situation from a different angle? Have you taken the time to define your career aspirations? Have you created a career development plan (see my book *Your Career, Your Way!* to learn how to create one) that includes actions you believe are needed to achieve your goals? Have you shared this information with your manager and asked for his or her help and support? What might seem like a reason to look for a different job could turn out to be something within your ability to control and change.

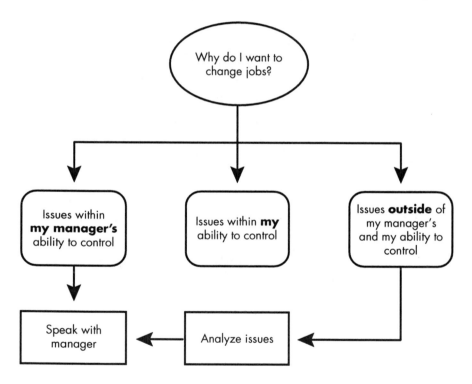

Let's look at another example of why you might want to leave your job – you're bored and want to do something more challenging. You might think this issue is outside your manager's and your control because, hey, it's the job, right? Wrong. Have you told your boss that you're bored and given him or her examples of the projects and tasks you'd like to take on to improve your skills and broaden your experience? Managers generally have a fair amount of discretion when it comes to allocating work to people they directly manage. Taking the time to talk through this with your manager might improve your situation enough that you won't need to look for a job elsewhere.

Maybe your reason for wanting a different job is related to coworkers, such as a colleague who keeps stealing your ideas or taking credit for your work. You might classify this as an issue within your manager's ability to control, or, if you've already approached your manager about the situation and it hasn't improved, then you might consider this as an issue falling outside your manager's or your control. But is it really?

Why do unethical people tend to steal ideas or credit only from certain people? Because they know they can get away with it. Looking for a different job because you don't want to deal with a coworker isn't a good reason to leave. Running away from difficult situations rarely works. Consider why you haven't already stood up for yourself and confronted the person. What is holding you back?

This particular problem kept happening to a client of mine. No matter where she worked or in what job, it seemed like there was always one person who would steal her ideas and claim them as his or her own. I told my client that until she addressed the issue by standing up for herself, this situation would likely continue. Once she became proactive and confronted the unethical coworker, guess what happened? The situation stopped.

The Universe has a funny way of working like that – until you learn how to deal with certain issues, they will continue. Once you've learned the life lesson, those types of situations tend to fade away. Changing jobs doesn't mean the issues will magically disappear, because those same situations could just as easily occur in your new job. As you consider *why* you want to change jobs and then analyze the issues to determine if they can be fixed, make sure your reasons for wanting to leave aren't related to avoiding a challenging problem.

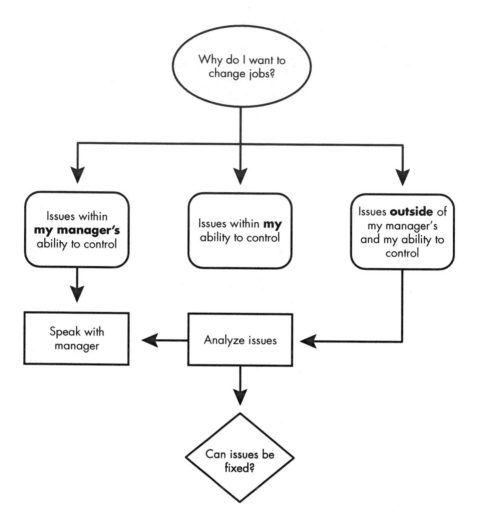

I also hear from many clients that they want to change jobs because they can't stand their boss. Are you really willing to veer off of your career path just because of a bad boss? Maybe a better route would be to learn techniques that will help you "manage up," until you can obtain a promotion or lateral move working under a different manager.

I once worked for a boss who turned out to be incredibly arrogant, unethical, and verbally abusive. Sure, one option was to simply find a different job at a different company. But I liked my job, I enjoyed working for the company, and I wanted to complete the work I had already begun in that role. I didn't want to let a bad manager change my career path or affect my goals, so I decided to remain in the job and try to work through the situation.

It wasn't easy, but when I look back on that time, I'm thankful for the experience. Going through that situation taught me professional and politically astute ways to stand up for my peers and myself. I became adept at dealing with difficult and emotionally challenged colleagues/managers. I also learned the process for handling someone who crosses ethical and legal boundaries at work. What I gained by staying in this position far surpassed what I would have learned by avoiding the bad boss and looking for a new job.

Could the same be said for many of the reasons you've provided for wanting to change jobs? If so, you could gain more experience from working through the issues. If you feel you're underpaid, try fixing the issue before looking for another job. Pull together salary research, along with a list of all your key projects and tasks, and then sit down with your manager for a discussion. If you want to learn new skills or improve weaknesses, talk with your manager to find out if there is a budget available for you to attend training courses, seminars, or classes. If your lengthy commute to work is lowering your quality of life, negotiate with your boss so you can work from home a few days a week.

No job is perfect and it is doubtful that you'll enjoy *every* aspect and every minute of your job – people rarely do. Maybe you're looking for more meaning or purpose in life and think you can find that through your work. Possibly. Or maybe you can find a hobby or perform volunteer work on the weekends that will bring you additional happiness and the purpose in life you're seeking. Changing jobs isn't the only answer – the key is taking time to understand why you want to change jobs and whether or not changing jobs is in your best interest.

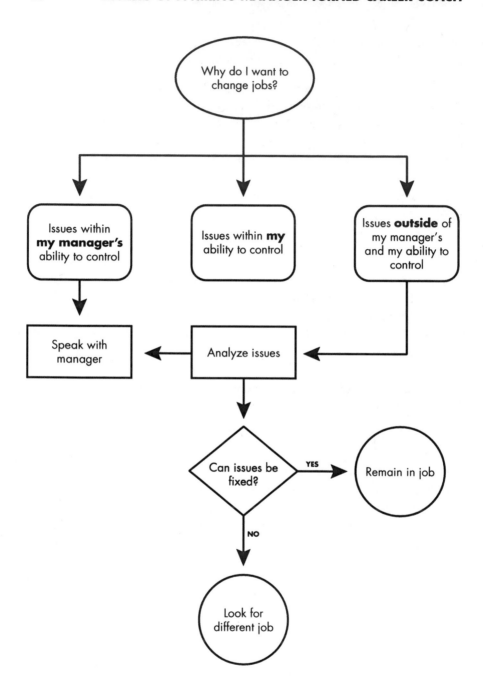

**CHAPTER 2
KEY TAKEAWAYS**

Before you jump into the job search process, take the time to consider why you want to look for a new job. Remember, no job is perfect. Categorize your reasons for wanting to change jobs so you can better understand which issues are within your manager's or your ability to control – only then will you be able to determine if changing jobs is in your best interest.

USE TEMPORARY WORK TO UNCOVER YOUR CAREER DIRECTION

Are you a recent high school or college graduate trying to decide on your career direction? Returning to work after taking time off to raise children or taking care of elderly parents, but not sure about the kind of work you'd like? Lost your job due to corporate downsizing and think it's time for a career change? Don't really like your job and wonder about other career options? If your situation falls into one of these categories then you might find it helpful to seek work at a temp agency. It could help you determine your career direction.

Temporary work agencies, also known as temp agencies or temp staffing firms, hire workers and then place them in assignments at other companies. Companies approach these temp agencies, define their worker needs, and then sign contracts for the agencies to supply the workers. These are usually full-time positions and can range from short-term, such as several weeks, to indefinite periods of time, such as six months and longer. Company placements can be in small start-ups all the way to multi-billion dollar global corporations.

In the past, temp agencies were known for supplying lower-skilled workers for entry-level type jobs. Today, most temp agencies provide highly skilled workers in a wide variety of industries and within many different job categories, such as: accounting and finance, call center and customer service, hospitality, marketing and communications, creative/graphic design, engineering, industrial and manufacturing, information technology, project management, process improvement, science, medical, transportation and warehousing, office and administrative.

If you are unsure about your career direction, working for a temp agency can provide you with an opportunity to try out different industries, companies, and jobs. By "trying on" different jobs, it makes it easier to figure out the jobs and companies you like and those you don't. That is what has happened with several of my clients.

Susan[1] had taken time away from her career to raise her children, but once her kids were in elementary school, she struggled to figure out the type of work that would make her happy. Working for a temp agency gave her the chance to try different jobs at a variety of companies and in several industries. Susan felt uncomfortable working in large companies with traditional office environments where she had to wear suits to work. That is how she came to realize her skills, personality, and work style were a better fit at smaller companies with casual and creative work environments. This realization helped Susan narrow her career direction. Then she found several small, local companies where she targeted her job search – eventually finding a job she really enjoyed.

Allie had recently graduated from college with a business degree, but couldn't decide which company she wanted to work for. So she went to work for a temp agency and specifically asked to be placed in different sized companies and in different industries. The opposite of Susan, Allie realized that she enjoyed working at large companies with traditional office environments. Even better, one of the companies was so impressed with Allie's skills and work ethic that they offered her a permanent position. *The result?* After only one year working for a temp agency, Allie turned her temp position into a permanent job.

When Deborah was let go due to corporate downsizing during the recession, she decided it was a good time to change careers. She had spent 15 years working in marketing for the same company and had become bored with the work. Deborah took a job working for a temp agency as a way to pay the bills. She also thought it would give her an opportunity to try working in different areas of business, which would help her identify her next career move. What she discovered was a surprise. Deborah realized she actually loved marketing work – she just needed a change into a different industry with

---

1. All of the stories in this book are true, but names have been changed throughout to protect my clients' privacy.

different products. *The result?* Deborah's creativity and marketing abilities were so impressive that two of the companies she temped at offered her permanent positions.

If you're trying to decide on your career direction or next career move, consider working for a temporary employment agency. Benefits:

- It gives you the opportunity to work for different sized companies with different cultural environments.
- It gives you the opportunity to work in different industries.
- It helps you learn new skills.
- It can help you update skills you haven't used in a while.
- It provides job experience you can add to your resume.
- It broadens your network of business contacts.
- It provides more people to use as job references.
- It helps get your foot in the door at your target companies.
- It is a great way to earn money, so you can pay bills.
- It often includes other benefits, such as medical insurance, sick pay, holiday pay, etc.
- Temporary work often leads to a full-time position.

**CHAPTER 3
KEY TAKEAWAYS**

If you're unsure about your career direction, working for a temporary agency can provide an opportunity to try out different industries, companies, and jobs. By "trying on" different jobs, it makes it easier to figure out the jobs and employers you like and those you don't.

CHAPTER 4

DEFINE YOUR CAREER ASPIRATIONS

When it comes to finding a job, have you ever felt like a cork bobbing in a stream, going wherever the current takes you? We've all been there at one time or another, but you probably won't end up where you want if you're simply floating with the current. Instead of relying on luck and hope, take control of your destiny by defining your career aspirations. Why? Because if you know where you want to go, it's a lot easier to figure out how to get there. Here are a few examples of this process in action.

Starting out in a new career

Amanda, one of my previous coaching clients, was a recent college graduate with an undergraduate degree in business. She had applied for all kinds of jobs and was going to a lot of interviews, but wasn't receiving any job offers. *Her problem?* Amanda hadn't taken the time to define her career aspirations, and without setting these she couldn't determine the specific actions needed to reach her career goals. She wasn't even sure what her career goals were! This meant Amanda's job search was unfocused and she spent a lot of time applying for positions she didn't know if she even wanted. In turn, this meant her interviews were also unfocused, and Amanda couldn't clearly articulate answers to many of the hiring managers' questions.

Recognizing that Amanda needed direction, we first discussed:

- Things that are important to her in life
- Work areas she feels she's good at
- Work areas she doesn't enjoy
- Her career aspirations

From this we determined that Amanda was most interested in the healthcare industry because of the time she had spent helping her younger brother with his medical issues. Amanda also identified that she was good at establishing long-term relationships, enjoyed working independently with little supervision, and wanted a job where she could be compensated for her efforts, not paid on an hourly basis. Even though Amanda didn't like her part-time college job in retail sales all that much, she *did* enjoy the challenge of selling and of achieving her sales goals and quotas.

This personal insight led us to look at the types of sales jobs available in the healthcare industry. This included everything from pharmaceutical sales to imaging equipment sales to medical equipment service agreement sales, consumables sales, dental equipment sales, implantable device sales, healthcare IT sales… and the list went on and on. After analyzing each type of sales opportunity, Amanda narrowed down her job aspiration list to two areas: pharmaceutical sales and dental equipment sales.

Once Amanda had determined two potential career areas, we went to work defining action items, including a timeline, which Amanda needed to complete before moving forward in her job search process. These included:

- Research available sales positions in the pharmaceutical industry
- Research available sales positions for dental equipment companies
- Contact her mother's friend, who was a pharmaceutical sales rep, and ask to spend a day or two on the job with her (job shadowing)
- Spend time at her dentist's office for informational interviews with her dentist and the dental hygienists to understand the dental sales industry from their perspective
- Contact several dental equipment sales companies and ask for an informational interview and a ride-along opportunity with a local sales representative (job shadowing)
- After completing the other action items, consider if one of the two areas is more appealing, pharmaceutical sales or dental equipment sales

At first, Amanda was surprised I had suggested job shadowing as a method to help her decide on her career direction. But job shadowing isn't just for kids – it is also for job hunters and career changers because it can be a great way to determine if a job will be a good fit with your background, skills, and areas of interest. Simply choose the key positions in which you're interested, schedule your job shadowing opportunities, and then see what it is like to be in those jobs. Find out what people already in the role like and dislike about their jobs, what it takes to be successful, and why they stay in their positions.

Amanda was able to job shadow her mother's friend (a pharmaceutical sales rep) for a few days as well as go on a ride-along with a local dental equipment sales rep. She spent a day at her dentist's office and was also able to obtain an informational interview with the sales manager of a dental equipment company. Her research and job shadowing helped Amanda realize her better choice would be starting out in a pharmaceutical sales role and then progressing into dental equipment sales later in her career, after she had obtained healthcare sales experience.

The result: Amanda accepted a job offer as a pharmaceutical sales representative. Over the next three years Amanda learned everything she could about the pharmaceutical industry and the products she represented. Amanda's success at building long-term relationships led to training responsibilities for new employees. Amanda now has many career opportunities available: she could become a pharmaceutical sales manager for a geographic region or a training manager for her current employer. Amanda could also use her pharmaceutical sales experience to obtain a job at a dental equipment sales company, should she choose to go that route in the future.

Changing careers

Defining aspirations and the action items needed to achieve them isn't just a technique to use when starting your career. This same technique can be applied to situations where you'd like to transition to a different job or industry or for securing a promotion.

Maureen is a great example of how beneficial this method can be at any age and at any stage in your career. Maureen was in her early 50s and almost every day she would stare out the window from her desk at work and dream about a different career.

She had stayed in her current job because it gave her steady work and she wanted a stable income while she and her husband raised their children. But now the kids were grown and she was letting herself think about a different career. She got excited just considering all the other job possibilities. *Her problem?* Maureen didn't know if the skills she had would translate into a different industry. Sound familiar?

I had Maureen complete the same exercise as Amanda – thinking about what is important to her and considering what she is good at and what she doesn't enjoy doing at work. From there, we created a list of actions for Maureen that would help her narrow down the industries and jobs that interested her.

In addition to the steps Amanda took, Maureen also spent time looking at the skills she had gained so far in her career and listed ways she could apply those same skills to her desired job. This action, paired with identifying her aspirations and action items, landed Maureen her dream job working in a different industry. And the bonus for her, she finally loved getting up every day to go to work.

Seeking a promotion

Do you already have a job but want to climb the career ladder into higher-level positions? Then let's examine Julia's situation. Julia was 35, married, and working in a sales position for a construction supply company. *Her problem?* Julia couldn't figure out why she was always getting passed over for promotion opportunities.

After we began talking about the same things I had discussed with Maureen and Amanda to uncover their career aspirations, Julia's problem and solution became very clear. Julia realized she had been waiting for others to offer her a promotion instead of defining the next job she wanted and determining the action items needed to obtain it. So Julia defined her next career goal and used my job seeker advice to guide her process for obtaining a promotion.

Julia was also able to recognize the areas she hadn't previously realized were holding her back and worked on improving her skills. And guess what? In a little over a year, she achieved her goal of becoming a sales manager.

If Julia, Maureen, and Amanda can follow this process to determine their career aspirations and develop a plan to reach them, so can you. Just remember, your dream job or ideal job may not be the job you get right now. You might have to spend time working your way up to that position, learning necessary skills, and gaining experience before you're qualified for the job. For example, after defining my aspirations and developing a career strategic plan, it took me 12 years until I finally earned my dream job: vice president of global marketing at a Fortune 500 company. Each job along the way enabled me to get one step closer to where I wanted to be and allowed me to gain the experience I needed to be successful in my dream job.

To get started mapping out your next career goal and the actions you'll take to achieve it, check out these **Appendix** templates at the back of the book (and online):

- **Aspiration Development (page 258)**
- **Action Item Definition (page 259)**

CHAPTER 4
KEY TAKEAWAYS

Don't rely on luck or hope when it comes to your career. Take control of your destiny by defining your career aspirations and then determining the specific actions needed to achieve them.

PART 2

EVALUATE JOBS AND YOUR SKILLS

RESEARCH COMPANIES AND INDUSTRIES

Once you've narrowed down your career aspiration to several jobs, the next step is to research the companies and industries where those jobs exist. Why should you spend time doing this homework? Because it will help you:

- Find out what companies exist in the industries in which you're interested.
- Discover which companies are hiring and for which positions.
- Determine if you're a good match for working at certain companies and vice versa.
- Sell yourself as the best job candidate during an interview.
- Prepare for difficult interview questions such as: *"Tell me what you know about our company and industry"* – which can bring an interview to a screeching halt if you haven't done your homework.
- Prepare interview questions to ask the hiring manager.

For each job you're interested in, go online and review the company's website. Spend time reading information about the products, services, company history, and even recent press releases. Write down or print out key information (or save it to your computer). Being a very analytical person, I actually enjoy this type of research, but realize not everyone does. If you don't like doing research and analysis, make yourself a cup of coffee, take a deep breath – *and do it anyway.* No matter how boring it seems, skipping this step will prevent you from obtaining a job that is a good fit. So ladies, I'm going to say it: Even if you hate conducting Internet research, you need to suck it up and do your homework.

If the company is publicly held, I always look for the latest annual report. These reports are incredibly useful because they're filled with most of the information you'll want to know, including: company overview, the names and background of the management team, the names and background of the Board members, key financial information (look at the year-over-year trends), issues the company is facing, their competitive strategy along with strategic, operational, and financial goals and objectives. There will also often be an explanation of the company's key products and services. Find this report (the most recent version), and you'll greatly cut down on the amount of time spent on research.

Here is the information you should try to find out about the company as you conduct your research:

Basic information: The company's legal name, website URL, office locations, and main office telephone number.

Size of company: Number of employees, total annual revenue, and revenue growth. Is the company in a fast-growing market or a mature and slow-growing market?

Age of company: Has the company been around for many years or is it still in a start-up phase?

Company history: Who started the company? Has the company acquired any other businesses or been acquired by another company?

Type of company: Is the company public or private, for profit or not-for-profit, a division of another company, etc.?

Products and/or services: What types of products or services are sold? Does the company manufacture them or subcontract the work?

Target market: Is the company business-to-business (B2B) or business-to-consumers (B2C). By this I mean, do they sell products and services to other companies, or, do they sell directly to end consumers, such as you and me? If the company sells to consumers, what are the consumer demographics?

Characteristics of customers (consumer demographics): Who typically purchases the products and services and what are the needs that are being fulfilled?

Key competitors: Who are they? Are there a few large competitors or a lot of small competitors?

Company culture, diversity, and environment: Will the company culture and environment fit your personality and work style?

Management: Who makes up the management team and board of directors? Do the teams include women and minorities (are they diverse)?

Recent news: What is the company saying about themselves in recent press releases? What are others saying about the company in news articles?

Community involvement: Is the company's workforce involved in any community outreach activities (volunteer work) or acts of corporate social responsibility?

Ethics: Has the company had any known issues or ethics violations? Check the Better Business Bureau website to research if there are any issues.

Business goals: What are the company's strategic goals and objectives (these are usually found in the annual report)?

While company websites are a great tool, they were created to make the company look good, so take the time to research a few additional resources. These might include:

- Hoover's Online: www.hoovers.com
- Vault: www.vault.com
- Wetfeet: www.wetfeet.com
- Online Yellow pages such as www.superpages.com or www.yellow.com
- Fortune 500 information: www.money.cnn.com/magazines/fortune/fortune500/
- 100 Fastest Growing Companies: www.money.cnn.com/magazines/fortune/fastest-growing/
- 100 Best Companies To Work For: www.money.cnn.com/magazines/fortune/best-companies/
- Top 50 Companies For Diversity: www.diversityinc.com/the-diversityinc-top-50-companies-for-diversity-2013 (or whatever year we're in)
- Online Finance programs, such as: www.finance.yahoo.com or www.google.com/finance

- Securities and Exchange Commission (for publicly held companies): www.sec.gov/
- Business Directories
- Local and National Newspapers
- Industry Journals
- Professional Journals
- Chambers of Commerce
- Analyst Reports
- State Government Websites
- Better Business Bureau
- Local Library (with experts who can guide you on where to find information)

After I've completed research on the company and industry, I also like to conduct online research about the hiring manager. If you know the hiring manager's name, you can look up their social media profiles (such as LinkedIn) or just type their name into a search engine and see what comes up. Things I look for are articles they may have written, awards won, or if they've been a guest speaker at any conferences. I also look at their educational background, work experience, and the progression of their jobs. As I mentioned earlier, job interviews should be a two-way street – so I like to conduct my own research on the hiring manager to help me determine if I'd want this person as my boss.

To assist you in your research homework, use the **Company Research Information (page 260)** template found in the **Appendix** at the back of this book (and online).

**CHAPTER 5
KEY TAKEAWAYS**

After determining the jobs that interest you, spend time researching the companies and industries where those positions exist. Bonus: the time you spend conducting research will also help prepare you for job interviews.

CHAPTER 6

RESEARCH AND ANALYZE JOB REQUIREMENTS

A few years ago I was holding in-person interviews for an available Marketing Manager position. I narrowed down the number of candidates after reviewing their resumes and conducting phone interviews. One person seemed especially promising, but during the interview it became clear that he hadn't even bothered to read the entire job description.

That told me he wasn't interested in the position. His lack of preparation also offered insight into what his work habits might be like. For example, I inferred he was probably the type of person who waited until the last minute to get things done, who didn't complete adequate research or analysis for projects, or who didn't anticipate questions that might be asked when presenting in front of groups.

Whether these were true or not, I kept conjuring up additional thoughts about the type of employee he might be. Needless to say, he didn't get the job. I was looking for someone who was far more prepared, ready to discuss the job requirements as they related to their experience and skills, and who had questions they wanted to ask to better understand the position.

This scenario shows why researching and analyzing the job requirements is such a big deal. When you fully understand the requirements, you can position yourself as the best possible candidate. But don't wait until the night before an interview to conduct this analysis. Download the job posting and carefully examine it before you even apply for the position.

This is an activity I helped my client Carol complete. She initially felt it was a waste of time until I pointed out that she hadn't included skills on her resume that were clearly stated in the job requirements of the position she wanted – skills I knew she had. Step-by-step, this is the process I laid out for Carol to follow to position herself as the best candidate.

First, carefully read the job description to make sure you fully understand it. Write notes in the margins of any questions you have for the hiring manager or items that are confusing, and highlight keywords used to describe the position and requirements.

Next, use this initial information to:

- Analyze your knowledge, skills, experience, and education to see how you compare to the job requirements and to identify gaps.
- Anticipate and prepare for the skill levels of other candidates.
- Brainstorm questions the interviewer could ask to find out how well you fit the requirements and practice your answers.
- Customize your resume to highlight your experiences that align with what the hiring manager is seeking (also known as "key wording" your resume).
- Customize cover letters to help differentiate yourself from other candidates.
- Determine clarifying questions to ask the interviewer if you don't understand a specific requirement.

The most important step is comparing or critically examining your skills with the job requirements to determine how you compare and if there are any gaps. To make this easier, I created a **Job Requirements Analysis (page 261)** sheet (you can find it in the **Appendix** at the back of the book and online) and asked Carol to fill out one sheet for each job.

In the column labeled, "Job Requirements," I had Carol write down each of the requirements listed on the job description, such as education, work experience, and specific skills. Next, she filled out the "My Analysis" section to compare her background against these requirements. Once Carol finished, the information showed us how her background and skills compared to the job requirements. I also had Carol look back at each job requirement and then write "Fully Meet," "Partially Meet," or "Don't Meet" next to each item – based on how she compared herself to the job requirements.

This is an important exercise every job seeker should complete *prior* to applying for a position. As Carol realized, there were certain job requirements where she had experience, but she had forgotten to include them on her resume – an easy update that could mean getting called for an interview.

There were also some skill requirements on the job posting that Carol didn't have. For the areas where she didn't meet or only partially met a requirement, we brainstormed ideas on how she could develop these skills. This included books she could read, classes or seminars she could attend, or ways she could learn the skill while working in the job. This helped her feel more prepared for job interviews and for potential questions about areas where she lacked experience. It also gave Carol some ideas for questions she could ask the hiring manager at the end of the interview to find out about potential training opportunities through that employer.

As a hiring manager, I always took time during interviews to review the job description and requirements with the candidate, asking how well he or she thought they met each requirement, based on their knowledge, skills, experience, or education.

As a job seeker, it is much easier to have this discussion if you've already followed the process I outlined. You'll be able to easily point to the areas on your resume that demonstrate your experience and you'll be comfortable discussing where there are gaps. I also recommend bringing your "Job Requirements Analysis" document to your job interview, show it to the hiring manager, and then walk him or her through each item. This shows you are:

- Taking the hiring process seriously.
- Making sure you fully understand the attributes and skills for which the employer is seeking.
- Ensuring the job is a two-way fit.
- Trying to anticipate areas in which you may not be a perfect fit, but that could then become growth areas.

Additionally, keep in mind there are usually more job applicants than available positions. That means to be successful you need to stand out from other candidates. Taking the time to review and understand the job description, analyze the job requirements against your experience, customize your resume, and then use your analysis to prepare for interviews is a great way to do this.

CHAPTER 6
KEY TAKEAWAYS

Take time to download, review, and understand the job description and to evaluate whether you meet the specific requirements. Then, use this information to customize your resume and to prepare for interviews. Doing so will help you differentiate yourself from other job seekers.

CHAPTER 7

CONDUCT A PERSONAL S.W.O.T. ANALYSIS

A valuable process companies use to assess themselves and their competitors to formulate their strategies is called a "S.W.O.T." analysis. A tried and true business technique, I have used the S.W.O.T. analysis for more than two decades for strategic planning. This exercise is also extremely helpful for job seekers and career ladder climbers.

Here is how the process works: After defining your career aspirations and evaluating your skill set against the job's requirements, the next step is to learn more about yourself and your external environment. S.W.O.T. stands for:

S = Strengths (internal)

W = Weaknesses (internal)

O = Opportunities (external)

T = Threats (external)

This analysis process is used to capture information about your internal strengths and weaknesses as well as external opportunities and threats. To get in the right mindset of completing a S.W.O.T. analysis, start thinking about your career like a business and yourself like a product.

Strengths. To help you understand your strengths, picture yourself as a competitive product. A personal strength is an asset to you as a product and can be used to differentiate yourself from others when interviewing or seeking your next promotion. A few examples of strengths: project management skills, ability to improve or reengineer processes, computer programming skills, experience presenting to large audiences, proven success achieving annual sales quotas.

Weaknesses. A personal weakness is a liability or an area for growth. These are characteristics you could improve to increase future job opportunities. A few examples of weaknesses: disorganized, tendency to procrastinate, poor at time management, uncomfortable speaking in front of groups, have never led a project or team, outdated computer skills.

Opportunities and Threats. When thinking about opportunities and threats, I always find it easier to begin with the "threats." Try comparing yourself to people you'll likely compete against for the job you want. Then, as objectively as possible, judge your threats (the competitive threats) and determine possible ways to overcome them (opportunities/initiatives). Here are some examples to help you understand the process.

Example 1:

Threat: The job description states that the position requires someone with a four-year college degree. Other candidates have college degrees, but I only have a two-year college degree.

Opportunity: I could go to night school and finish my four-year college degree. Or, during job interviews, I could discuss how my four years of work experience is equivalent to the college degree requirement.

Example 2:

Threat: The higher-level job I want requires training large groups of employees, but I'm not very good at public speaking.

Opportunity: I could take a speech class in the evenings or join a program, such as Toastmasters. I could also seek out opportunities to improve my presentation skills, such as asking my manager if I could provide a training session during an upcoming department staff meeting.

The purpose of the personal S.W.O.T. analysis is to identify steps you can take to best meet the requirements of the job or promotion you want, or to find ways around them. Comparing your strengths and weaknesses to the job requirements will help you identify gaps and better prepare you for the job interview as well as the position.

Here are two completed examples using Mackenzie and Cheryl.

Mackenzie's completed S.W.O.T. Analysis:

STRENGTHS (ASSETS)	WEAKNESSES (LIABILITIES)
• Creative • Goal oriented • Expressive • Risk taker • Confident • Decisive	• No MBA degree • Uncomfortable speaking before large groups • Could be more organized • Tends to take on too many projects/unreliable • Poor listener • Sometimes too casual in appearance • Procrastinates • Judgmental of others/doesn't always listen to what others are saying
THREATS (COMPETITOR STRENGTHS)	**OPPORTUNITIES (INITIATIVES)**
• Others hold MBA Degrees • Others have extensive business experience • Others consistently meet and exceed objectives • Others have international business experience • Others complete projects on time • Others are comfortable presenting in front of a large audience • Others have experience managing and motivating personnel • Others dress more professionally	• Research MBA programs at colleges and universities in her area. Determine costs and time to complete. Consider night school. • Continue to work and advance in the field of marketing. Identify incremental promotional steps. • Take classes on time and project management. • Seek out participation on future international projects • Take on fewer projects to complete prior commitments on time. • Take a speech class and consider taking an acting class. • Take some classes on effectively managing people. Seek out promotional opportunities that would provide experience in managing others. • Seek help from an image consultant.

Cheryl's completed S.W.O.T. Analysis:

STRENGTHS (ASSETS)	WEAKNESSES (LIABILITIES)
• Work experience (10 years) • Retail knowledge	• No college degree • Lack of knowledge and experience managing a budget • Low confidence level in proactively leading projects

THREATS (COMPETITOR STRENGTHS)	OPPORTUNITIES (INITIATIVES)
• Others have Bachelor's Degrees • Others have experience with budgets • Others are more proactive and assertive • John has a degree and strengths in almost all the position requirements	• Ongoing education through classes and seminars • Sign up for and complete seminar on "Finance for the Non-Financial Manager" • Proactively meet with hiring manager • Proactively meet with boss to secure support and demonstrate my desire to take on this new role • Complete the opportunities listed above and demonstrate that through my 10 years of working, I have gained on-the-job experience equivalent to or exceeding that of a college degree

Throughout my career, I've used the S.W.O.T. analysis every time I've applied and interviewed for a job. Going through this exercise has ensured I'm prepared for the interview and gets me ready to answer tough questions from hiring managers, such as, *"Describe your biggest weakness"* (no one wants to get caught without an answer to this one!). Following this process also allows me to anticipate areas that could be potential issues during the interview, so I can determine ahead of time how to respond.

In my own career, when I am in job interviews (as the candidate), I often explain to the hiring manager the process I've gone through to ensure I'm qualified for the position. I will even show him or her my S.W.O.T. analysis.

Hiring managers have always been impressed with the homework I've done and the thought I've put in to make sure the job is a good fit for my knowledge, experience, skills, education, and personality type.

As you go through this process yourself, here are helpful tips for completing the S.W.O.T. analysis exercise:

- Choose a location that is comfortable and quiet.
- Approach this exercise with a fresh mindset. Clear your mind and be relaxed and refreshed before you start. If you've had a bad day, this is definitely not the time to work on this exercise.
- Write down your thoughts as quickly as possible.
- Avoid the tendency to be overly critical of yourself in the "Weaknesses" category.
- View yourself as a competitive product and have some fun creating your list.
- Remember, there are no wrong answers.

After you've gone through the S.W.O.T. exercise, seek out a few people who know you well and ask them to review it and provide feedback. Do they agree with your strengths and weaknesses? In other words, do the perceptions of others equal your opinion of yourself? In life, perception is often reality. It is as true with people as it is with consumer products. As you begin to *think about your career as a business and yourself as a product,* make sure you take time to understand how others perceive you. Then, you'll be in a much better position to know where and how to focus your time and efforts to make the right changes or enhancements to your product (you).

To make completing a personal **S.W.O.T. analysis (page 262)** even easier, you can find a template in the book's **Appendix** (and online).

CHAPTER 7
KEY TAKEAWAYS

Because it encourages self-improvement, using a personal S.W.O.T. analysis to evaluate yourself and your competition will keep you at your best. Use the exercise to sharpen your strengths, improve your weaknesses, identify opportunities for development, and neutralize or overcome your threats.

PART 3

DEVELOP YOUR DOCUMENTS

CHAPTER 8

PREPARE YOUR RESUME

Your resume is typically the first item a potential employer will see. This means it needs to be the best advertisement possible, selling you as the best candidate for the job. Just how do you do that? Read on to find out.

First, what exactly is a resume?

A resume is a document that lists, very concisely, your job experience, skills, accomplishments, and education. The term resume is often used interchangeably with "curriculum vitae" or "CV"; however, a CV is more often used in the medical and academic environments and tends to contain much more in-depth education and publication information. For the purposes of this book, we'll use the term "resume."

What should you include?

A resume header: With your name and contact information (email address, phone number, and if applicable, mailing address). Also consider including the URL to your LinkedIn profile.

Skills Summary (optional): If you have a long work history, some find it helpful to include a skills summary statement or bulleted list of skills that are directly related to the job for which you are applying. You should place this section just under your header. *Here is an example of a skills summary statement:* "Experienced business development manager with extensive background in mergers and acquisitions, process reengineering, and operational restructuring and improvement. Accustomed to working with executive-level management teams with varying personalities."

Education: Include relevant information like the name of your college or university with city and state, degree(s) obtained (or working towards) and optionally your graduation year and grade point average. If you are at the beginning of your career, list your education first. If you have five or more years of work experience, list that first.

Experience: The name of each company or organization with city and state, your title, dates of work (include the month and year), and your key accomplishments in each position.

Skills (optional): Most skills should be demonstrated through your accomplishments listed under each job (or in a "Skills Summary" after your contact information); however, many people in IT use a separate section after their "Experience" to list specific programming skills, like SQL, Java, HTML, JavaScript, C++, XML, C#, C, Perl, Python, PHP, etc.

Community Service (optional): If you have volunteer work experience that specifically relates to the job you're seeking, you could include it in a "Community Service" or "Volunteer Work" section. This can be helpful, especially for job seekers new to the workforce or for those returning to work after taking time off to raise children. Use this section to demonstrate the experience and skills you've gained through your volunteer efforts and be prepared to discuss how these relate to the position when you're in the job interview.

Association Memberships (optional): If memberships are work-related, consider including this information in a separate section. For example, if you are an engineer you might list that you're a member of the Society of Women Engineers (SWE). If you're an accountant and a member of the American Society of Women Accountants (ASWA) you could include that organization. If you're in the field of marketing, you might want to list that you're a member of the Association for Women in Communications (AWC). Including relevant memberships can help demonstrate to hiring managers that you're active in your work community and stay up-to-date with industry information or changes.

Taking a resume from lackluster to standout

Jessica was a client experiencing difficulty obtaining job interviews. She applied online for several positions, but wasn't getting call backs for interviews. So we met at a local coffee shop for pumpkin spice lattes (yes, *with* whipped cream), and I analyzed her resume. *Her problem?* Jessica's resume was almost six pages long. She had mistakenly subscribed to the idea that "more is better" and included as much information as possible.

Jessica had also included a "Job Objective" paragraph at the beginning of her resume. This paragraph stated: "To obtain a job that will allow me to best utilize my skills and abilities for a company that will allow me to learn and grow..." On and on it went. This was a generic, "doesn't mean much of anything" paragraph that didn't add any value to her resume and took up a lot of space.

As a hiring manager, these "Job Objective" sections always made me wonder about the job candidate. *Were they not previously using their skills? Were they not previously working at a company that allowed them to learn and grow?* As we discussed my dislike for "Job Objective" sections on resumes, Jessica realized that what she had written was actually nothing more than a "fluff" paragraph. It had no content that would be helpful to a hiring manager and was wasting valuable space on her resume.

Next, we addressed the length of Jessica's resume. Given the number of years she had worked, it was far too long. Why was her resume so long? Jessica had used the HR job descriptions for all of her positions, which are often lengthy, instead of briefly explaining her key accomplishments in each job. Avoid this!

Instead, use bullets to itemize your key accomplishments and try to quantify the impact of your work as much as possible. Most hiring managers, once they read your title, will have a good understanding of your job; focusing on your key accomplishments in each position is what will set you apart.

Here is an example of how we changed Jessica's resume to highlight her accomplishments:

- *Old:* Led a process improvement project for invoicing.
- *New:* Led a process improvement project, which resulted in decreasing invoicing errors by 22%.

Over the next hour, we made these changes throughout Jessica's resume. By clearly defining the value Jessica contributed to each position, she helped hiring managers envision the unique skills she could bring to the job.

Other changes we made

Included her college grade point average. Jessica's grade point was very high and she had also worked full-time while putting herself through college. This could help differentiate Jessica as a hard worker who was disciplined in her studies.

Fixed all spelling errors and grammar. I cannot emphasize enough the importance of having an error-free resume. Most hiring managers quickly look at a resume and if it is filled with errors, they'll toss the resume into the garbage. They assume that a resume filled with errors means the person's work will likely follow suit.

Put her jobs in reverse chronological order – from current (or most recent) first to oldest job last.

Ensured key words from the job description were included. Remember all the work you did from Chapter 6: Research and Analyze Job Requirements? I had Jessica complete the same exercise, and where she met the requirements, we included those in her resume.

Changed the font type and font size. Jessica had used several different font types that were fairly unique styles and many different sizes throughout her resume. However, it is best not to get too fancy, so use a common font, and then use that same font style throughout your resume. If you want to use more font styles, limit yourself to one additional font - for your name, so it will stand out at the top of page one. While the size of your fonts might differ (largest size font for your name, slightly larger font size for section headings), never use a font size smaller than 10 point. Try to keep your resume fonts to between 10-12 points (your name can be larger sized).

Changed her email address. Jessica had a personal email address she thought was cute: *ilovetennis@gmail.com.* While it might sound cute to friends who know Jessica, it was unprofessional as a contact email address for work purposes. I had Jessica create a new email account for her job search: *Jessica_lastnamehere50@ gmail.com,* which we then used in her contact information at the top of her resume. Always use a professional-looking email account for your job search. The best email to use is: firstname.lastname@tbdprovider.com. Avoid unprofessional, cutesy, and potentially offensive nicknames, such as: *hippygirl17@*

aol.com, glittergal@yahoo.com, fairyprincess@tbd.com, sexymamma@tbd.com...
you get the idea.

Changed her voicemail message. Jessica was surprised when I called her mobile phone while we were sitting together in the coffee shop. I told her to let it ring and go into voicemail. That's because I wanted to hear her voicemail message. It wasn't a bad message, but there was a lot of background noise and it sounded like she might have recorded her message while standing in the check out line at a store. Unfortunately, public places aren't the best locations to record your cell phone greeting. That evening, I had Jessica record a new message while sitting at home – with no background noise. Always make sure you listen to your voicemail message and, if need be, record a new, professional-sounding message *before* you begin applying for jobs.

Should you ever stretch the truth?

After we double-checked Jessica's resume against the job description, we discussed one area where she did not fully meet the requirements. She asked me, *"Should I stretch the truth a little bit?"*

I gave her the same response I tell all my clients: *"While it is important not to undersell yourself, never lie or stretch the truth on your resume."* The Internet and other technologies have made it easier than ever to detect embellishments and lies. Companies you've worked for, dates of employment, job titles, job responsibilities, universities attended, and academic degrees can be quickly verified. Plus, lies can be easily uncovered during interviews.

For example, whenever I interview someone I purposely spend time discussing their accomplishments in various jobs. If the candidate stated on their resume that they saved company XYZ $7 million last year, then I start digging deeper for more information. *What did you do to save the company money? Did you lead the project or just participate in it? Who were the key stakeholder groups? Who was your project sponsor? What barriers did you run into during the project and how did you overcome them?* etc. If someone is lying about their accomplishments, they'll have a difficult time answering these kinds of in-depth questions. By asking the right questions, it is easy for an experienced hiring manager to figure out when a candidate is lying or stretching the truth about their skills or experience.

The other popular question I'm asked typically comes from older workers who consider leaving work experience off their resume. One woman inquired during a resume-writing seminar: *"I'm applying for a position at a company where the average employee age is 30. I'm 52 and would be working for someone much younger than I am, and I don't want them to say that I'm overqualified. I really want to work at this start-up company, but I'm worried they'll think I'm too old. Should I leave the first 10-15 years of my career off of my resume?"*

If this is a concern, one way to avoid showing your age on a resume is to omit the dates of your education, omit the job(s) you held during college, and omit the first few jobs after you graduated. Many hiring managers and recruiters will tell you that work experience older than 15-20 years tends to be irrelevant or less important, because so many things about business will have changed. Keep older job accomplishments brief and use the majority of your resume to demonstrate your achievements in your most recent positions (as they pertain to the job you want).

> Avoid the functional resume format unless it is a requirement as part of the job application process.

Another way job candidates sometimes try to get around the age issue is by creating a functional resume, which focuses on skills and experience instead of listing jobs by chronological order. The problem with this type of resume is that it tends to be atypical and can be confusing to hiring managers. Typically hiring managers and recruiters want to review the various jobs you've held, discuss how you progressed through them, and find out what you learned and/or accomplished in each position. This is difficult to do when looking at a functional resume, so my advice is to avoid the functional resume format unless it is a requirement as part of the job application process.

If you use any of these approaches, make sure you're smart about how you implement them. A hiring manager doesn't need a genius IQ to notice when something seems strange between the resume and the person sitting in front of them. For example, I once interviewed a woman whose resume work history showed a total of 12 years in length. Yet the woman sitting in front of me was obviously in her late 50s. Turns out, she had purposely not included more than half of her work experience because she thought her age would prevent her from getting the position. It didn't.

As I dug deeper into her work history and achievements, I discovered that much of it was directly applicable to the job for which she was interviewing. Smart recruiters and hiring managers know that finding the best person for the job has nothing to do with age, and they look for the person with the best background, skills, education, and attitude to fit the position. If you are an older worker, be proud of your work experience and focus on highlighting your key accomplishments as they relate to the job you seek.

The biggest issue I've had when interviewing older candidates is a lack of technology and computer skills. This can become a problem even if you already have a job. For example, a male manager's lack of computer skills meant the company he worked for had been providing him with a full-time assistant to help him with his computer work. He was a long-term employee and this situation had been going on for many years. But when the economy crashed and the company was forced to downsize, both the manager and his assistant were let go.

The reality? Other workers were available who had the technology savvy and computer skills to do the same job as the two employees combined. So if you're an older worker and you want to remain a valuable entity in the job market, take actions each year to ensure you keep up with your computer skills and with technological advances.

What to do before hitting send

After you're done creating or updating your resume, carefully read through it once, looking for spelling errors. Then read it a second time, checking the spelling and grammar. Most importantly, read it a third time to ensure that all the content makes sense. Ask yourself, *"Does my overall theme or career 'story' come across?"* Your career story is the narrative that explains your professional life. Humans tend to best communicate through the use of stories, so treat each job as a "chapter" in your career story to highlight experiences and accomplishments that will appeal to hiring managers.

Next, ask three friends or family members to read your resume and provide you with suggestions for improvement. After that, review your resume once a quarter (every three months) and keep it updated. At a minimum, update it once per year – and save all previous versions.

Electronic titling of your resume

Finally, carefully title your electronic resume so when you upload it or attach it to an email, it will be easy for a recruiter or hiring manager to know whose resume it is. Use your name, the job title, company, and date you apply (using the international date format). To keep the document title from being too long, abbreviate where possible. Let's say your name is Jane Doe and you're applying for the position of Marketing Communications Manager at a company named Acme, Incorporated. Here is how you would title your electronic resume: Jane Doe Resume_MarCom Mgr_Acme, Inc_15Sept2014

This electronic document titling format will also make it easier for you to keep track of all versions of your resume, since you'll be creating a customized resume for every job you apply to. With one look at the document title, you'll know when you applied, the name of the position, and for what company. See how helpful that is?

A quick reminder... always carefully follow the instructions when you apply online. You might be required to upload your resume as a PDF document or as a Word document. In some cases, you might be required to copy information from your resume and paste it into separate areas of the online application tool. If no resume format is specified, always convert your resume into a PDF document before uploading it, so your formatting and page breaks will remain intact. Once you've converted your resume into a PDF document, open the file and review it to ensure it looks okay before you upload it.

Read the instructions thoroughly and then follow them *exactly* as you apply online – because you never know when the employer will include an odd request. For example, after uploading a PDF of her resume and cover letter online, one client was asked to provide the name of the capital city for an obscure country. Employers make these requests to eliminate candidates who don't follow instructions. Don't be someone who gets eliminated!

Use the following (and online) templates at the back of this book to help you create your resume:

- **Resume Example #1 (page 263):** Provides an example resume for someone just beginning their career (Jane Doe 1)

- **Resume Example #2 (page 264):** Provides an example resume for someone already several years into their career (Jane Doe 2)
- **Resume Example #3 (page 265):** Provides an example resume that includes a "Skills Summary" section at the beginning (Jane Doe 3)
- **Resume Tips (page 266):** Use this as a checklist of things to consider before you submit your resume online

CHAPTER 8
KEY TAKEAWAYS

A resume is the best advertisement of YOU, so spend adequate time making it the best it can be. A good resume will help you get your foot in the door, and that is the best way to lead to a job interview.

ADDRESS RESUME GAPS

Early in my career, my manager asked me to participate on the interview panel for an open position in our department. Towards the end of the interview (which had been going fairly well), the coworker to my left said to the candidate, *"I noticed there is a two-year time period where you don't list any jobs on your resume. Since I don't see any volunteer work during this time, I was wondering what you were doing during that gap in your resume."*

The candidate's face turned ghostly white and it looked like he might throw up. Then he stared at his shoes and sighed. When he looked back up at the panel, he replied, *"The job I had right before that two-year period was incredibly stressful. I ended up having a mental breakdown and, after I got out of the hospital, I took two years off to travel around Europe and find myself."*

Wow. You could have heard a pin drop in that conference room. Talk about being honest. When I looked over at the HR manager, I could tell from the horrified look on her face that the candidate had shared too much information. At that time, I didn't yet know about all the various topics interviewers and candidates should avoid discussing during job interviews, such as physical, mental, or sensory disabilities, race, religion, gender, age, national origin, marital status, sexual orientation, gender expression or identity, and veteran or military status. These are all "protected classes" under most U.S. state laws.

His explanation of his two-year gap made my heart ache for what he'd been through, yet at the same time, it made me uncomfortable. What I learned after the interview is that, while the question my coworker had asked about the resume gap was legal, the candidate's answer had ventured into an area that he hadn't needed to discuss. Because of this specific situation, I began paying close attention to gaps in resumes, and to how candidates explained those gaps.

What I learned as a hiring manager and from working with many other hiring managers and HR personnel might surprise you – that having a gap on a resume isn't as big of a deal as most people would think. For example, after the economy crashed in the 2008-2009 time frame, I rarely saw a resume that didn't have a gap, because so many employees around the world had been laid off due to corporate downsizing. With so many people available for a smaller amount of open positions, it made it even harder for high school and college graduates to obtain jobs right after school – further increasing the number of people with gaps on their resumes.

There can be many reasons why you might have a gap in your resume, such as:

- Being laid off due to corporate downsizing.
- Lack of availability of jobs after high school or college.
- Taking time out to raise children.
- Taking time out to care for sick relatives or elderly parents.
- Taking a sabbatical.
- Taking time off to go back to school full-time.
- Taking time off for medical reasons.
- Taking time off for military work (which I wouldn't technically classify as a gap in a resume, because it is still a type of work).

For all my clients who took time off from their careers to raise children, their biggest worry was how that gap would be perceived by recruiters and hiring managers. What I've found is that a gap in their resume made very little difference in obtaining an interview. What mattered more is how they explained the gap, be it in their resume, cover letter, telephone interview, or in-person interview.

Amy was a client who had taken time off to raise her two children. Once they were in elementary school, she decided to re-enter the workforce, but was feeling uncomfortable with how she should explain the almost seven-year gap in her resume. During this time, Amy had stayed active with volunteer work and had even served as president of the parent-teacher-student association (PTSA) at her children's school for four years.

The solution? On her resume, we created a section titled "Community Service," which we placed right after her "Job Experience" section and clearly noted her dates of service. We also practiced how Amy would discuss her time away from work by focusing on the volunteer service projects she led and the results she achieved, as well as her accomplishments as the PTSA President. What surprised Amy the most was that, during job interviews, the gap turned out to be a non-issue.

Angela was another client who had also taken time out of her career – she had been raising three energetic boys. Angela thought she had a gap of many years in her resume, but I saw her situation differently. During the time Angela was at home raising their children, she had taken on all of the back-office duties for her husband's small business. She was handling everything from website creation and maintenance to payroll and order processing, business tax payments, and invoicing. Angela was even training all the new employees and answering customer calls every day. She wasn't getting paid for her work, but it was definitely experience Angela could include on her resume.

Angela laughed when I asked what her job title was for all the work she did for her husband's company. I told her I was serious. Then I asked what her husband was going to do when Angela found another job and wouldn't be able to help him anymore. *"I guess he'll finally have to hire himself an office manager,"* she replied. So we wrote up a job description for all of the work she did for her husband's company, and we included this work experience on her resume in a "Volunteer Work" section. We also practiced how she would answer interview questions in case any came up about the gap in her resume.

By the time Angela went on job interviews, she was able to easily explain what she had been doing while raising their children. She also made sure she pointed out how she would be able to use this experience in the new job. As with Amy, the gap in Angela's resume turned out to be a non-issue for hiring managers, and she soon received several job offers.

Even if you didn't have time for volunteer work while you raised your children, there are still skills you learned or improved upon that are transferable to the workplace. Were your kids in sports or other activities? Then I bet you further developed your ability to prioritize and also improved your time management skills. Were you in charge of your family's budget and major household purchases? Budget creation and management are important business skills. Raising children also tests your negotiation abilities, improves your conflict management skills, and, most likely, tested your communication skills on a daily basis.

Further, supervising children's activities and playgroups requires many of the same skills as supervising project teams or groups in workplace situations – the ability to manage conflicts, remain calm under pressure, work with different personality types, delegate responsibilities, provide effective feedback, multi-task, even make and implement decisions. All of these skills can be used to demonstrate why you're qualified for the job you're seeking.

Do's and Don'ts for handling work gaps

DO:

- Acknowledge to yourself that you have a resume gap and then take a deep breath and try to relax – really, it is not as big a deal as you might think.
- Analyze what you were doing during the gap. Could it be included on your resume as additional experience you gained, even if you weren't paid for your services?
- Use your cover letter to briefly explain your employment gap, if you're worried the gap will be an issue.
- Be prepared to discuss the work gap during job interviews. What did you do during that time? What new skills did you learn or improve upon? What did you do to stay current on what is happening in the industry? Did you attend any classes, courses, or seminars? Did you obtain any additional college credits, degrees, or certifications? Did you perform any volunteer work?
- Address any employment gaps honestly, but make sure you understand your legal rights as to the topics you DON'T have to discuss (such as those falling into "protected classes" or under equal opportunity employment rules).

DON'T:

- Use a functional resume format (explaining skills) instead of a traditional resume format (listing jobs in reverse chronological order) merely to try and hide employment gaps. Good hiring managers and recruiters always see through these attempts and it could keep you from getting the job. Instead, add a "Skills Summary" section at the beginning of your resume (before your "Work Experience" section) to draw the recruiter and hiring manager's attention to the key skills you would bring to the position.

- Omit employment dates or state only the years of employment in an attempt to hide employment gaps. Ask any hiring manager or recruiter and he or she will tell you that omitting dates or providing only employment years (such as 2006-2009) is a dead giveaway that a job candidate is trying to hide employment gaps. Including the months and years of work history has become a requirement, not an option. For example, whenever I have a candidate or a client who lists only the employment years, I specifically ask the person to provide the month information. Keep in mind that past employment (months and years) is verified as part of the background check process (often called "Employment History Verification"), so the employer will eventually find out anyway.

- Use the term "sabbatical" as a way to cover up gaps in employment. A sabbatical is a paid leave of absence from an employer. Use this term only if it is the true reason for why you were away from work and be able to speak to what you did/accomplished during your sabbatical.

- Lie on your resume about employment gaps. It doesn't take long to contact previous employers to verify past jobs, titles, and employment dates. Finding out a candidate lied on their resume (or lied by omission) is a quick way to get eliminated from the hiring process.

Ways to address gaps in a cover letter

Trying to determine the best way to handle an employment gap in your cover letter? Here are a few examples:

Stay-at-home mom, returning to work: "As you will see from my enclosed resume, I have a Master's degree in Education and spent eight years as a third grade teacher in the XYZ School District. After taking a six-year leave from teaching to raise our children, I went back to work last year as a substitute teacher. I am excited to pursue this full-time teaching job in…"

Obtaining a job after a layoff: "After five years working as a business analyst for ABC Company, my position was eliminated due to corporate downsizing. After the layoff, I used my time away from work to obtain my CPA certification and took classes to increase my computer skills. My goal is to use my experience as an analyst and the knowledge I gained through my CPA program to obtain the position of TBD in the Accounting and Finance department at…"

Obtaining a job after taking time off for college: "With seven years of experience in marketing, I took time out of my career to go back to school full time and completed my MBA in Marketing at the University of XXX. While in school, I worked as a paid intern for two companies in the area of product management – and ended up finding my career passion. I look forward to being able to use the knowledge and skills I've learned by applying them to the newly created position of Product Manager, XYZ product line, for Acme, Incorporated…"

Addressing a different kind of gap – just graduated from school

If you've recently graduated from high school or college, you might wonder what to include on your resume if you don't have paid work experience at multiple companies. In this situation, look for any work you've done which could demonstrate that you're a responsible, trustworthy adult. Consider including experience such as baby-sitting or working as a nanny and any other work you might have done around your neighborhood, even lawn mowing jobs or helping care for elderly neighbors.

Volunteer work might not have been paid, but it is still useful experience to include on your resume. For example, have you been a volunteer at a local hospital, nursing home, or senior center? Have you completed any volunteer work for organizations such as the United Way, your local Food Bank, the Humane Society, March of Dimes, American Heart Association, Susan G. Komen, Habitat for Humanity, Make a Wish Foundation, YWCA or YMCA, etc.? If yes, include this information and your responsibilities/accomplishments on your resume.

You could also include information about school projects on which you worked and positions you held in school activities or clubs, such as vice president of the senior class, manager of the student store, president of honor society, captain of a sports team, secretary for DECA, competitive member of Mathletes, member of the debate team, etc. List the club, your position, and then include what you did (responsibilities) and what you accomplished. If you can quantify your results, even better! For example, if you were the manager of the student store, did you introduce any new products or promotions that increased revenue? If yes, include that information in your resume, such as: "Introduced new line of healthy snacks and drinks, increasing student store revenue +17%."

Remember, while employment gaps might have been seen as unusual in the past, gaps are now fairly common, due to the economic recession, so use that to your advantage. Think through the best ways to address any gaps and then show up at job interviews prepared to discuss what you did and what you accomplished during your time away from work.

CHAPTER 9
KEY TAKEAWAYS

Having a gap on a resume isn't as big of a deal as you'd think. What matters more is how you explain the gap, be it in your resume, cover letter, telephone interview, or in-person interview. Analyze what you were doing during the gap to see if you could include it on your resume (even if it was unpaid/volunteer work). Then, be prepared to discuss the work gap during job interviews.

CHAPTER 10

PREPARE YOUR LIST
OF REFERENCES

A group of college students I was mentoring at the local university stared at me with questioning looks on their faces. One student raised her hand. *"But I thought I only had to come up with a reference list if I made it to the final interview and they asked me for it. Isn't it a waste of time to create it before it's needed?"*

"While waiting to create your list of references until after you've been asked for it is an option, my recommendation is that you create your list right after you create or update your resume," was my response. *"Because if you wait until you're asked for it, it might be too late."*

Creating your reference list and obtaining each person's permission to use him or her as a reference often takes a little time. That is the main reason for proactively creating a reference list before you even begin applying for jobs. The other reason is that you never want to be caught sitting in a job interview being asked for something you cannot readily hand to the hiring manager or HR recruiter. This is a quick way to get knocked out of the hiring process.

Most hiring managers or HR personnel will first contact your previous employers to verify past jobs, titles, and employment dates. After that, they will use your reference list to contact your professional and personal references. I've found that the majority of companies ask for three references, so include at least three, but no more than five. That way, there are enough references just in case someone can't be reached in a timely manner, but not so many as to look overwhelming on your document.

Your list should mainly include professional references, such as former bosses, coworkers, direct reports, clients or customers, or vendors. Professional references are just that, people with whom you've had a business relationship. If you're just beginning your career and don't have enough professional references, you can use one or two personal references. These are sometimes also called character references and include people who know you well, such as former college professors or high school teachers, past athletic coaches, leaders of community service organizations where you've been a volunteer, and long-time family friends and neighbors. Avoid using immediate family members (such as your mom, dad, sister, or brother) as personal references.

When creating your reference list, potential references may be approached in person, by telephone, email, or via social media account messaging. My personal preference has always been to contact people by telephone, but you will know the individuals the best, so choose the most appropriate method for each person.

Here are tips for contacting potential references:

- Let the person know that you're searching for a new job and creating a list of references.
- Ask if they know you well enough to feel comfortable serving as a reference.
- Let them know about the type(s) of jobs for which you're seeking and why these jobs are of interest.
- If the person says yes, let them know you would like to verify their contact information to ensure accuracy and to make sure you are *only* providing information with their permission.
- If they are unable to act as a reference, don't get defensive. Some people may feel uncomfortable being a reference. Be polite, be professional, and thank them for their time and consideration.
- For all those who said yes, send them a thank you note (either handwritten or electronic) letting them know how much you appreciate their willingness to serve as a reference and that you will keep them updated on your job search progress.

When you speak with each person who agrees to serve as a reference, here is the information you should obtain from him or her to include on your reference list:

- The person's full name (verify the spelling of their first and last names).
- Their title.
- The name of the company for which they work.
- The company's mailing address.
- The person's email address.
- The person's telephone number.
- Their relationship to you (such as former manager, former coworker, former direct report, etc.).

In the **Appendix** section, see the **Reference List (page 268)** for an example of the document you'll need to create.

As I worked with Megan to help with her job search, I saw that she had already created a reference list. *Her problem?* Megan's reference list only contained three names – and they weren't business references, they were all personal friends, even though she had more than five years of work experience.

While it was admirable that Megan had friends willing to help, hiring managers and HR personnel generally use reference lists to verify qualifications of the job applicant and to further explore areas of expertise or experience. This can be difficult to do if you only include personal references. Because of this, it is best to look for references with whom you've worked in a business capacity.

It has been my experience that the preference of hiring managers, recruiters, and other HR personnel is to first speak with previous managers who were responsible for writing your performance appraisals and who are familiar with your strengths and weaknesses as well as your work habits and communication style. This could be previous supervisors or managers, or if you were a summer intern, it could be the intern coordinator or the manager to whom you were assigned. If you were a volunteer for a local charity, it could be the person for whom you completed the community service work.

I had Megan brainstorm a list of potential professional references. These included former bosses, several former coworkers, and the director of a local charity where Megan had volunteered for the past two years. After speaking with each person, her final list included five people: Two former managers, two former coworkers, and the charity director. This is a nice mix of people, as it will allow any person checking Megan's references to gain a good overall picture of her work experience, skills, and interaction with others from several different perspectives.

Do's and Don'ts when you create your list of references

DO:

- Use the same style, layout, font(s), and font size as your resume.
- List your references in this order: managers, coworkers, direct reports, and then personal references last.
- Provide enough white space in between each person's information to be able to easily read the information and for the reference checker to write notes as they speak with each person.
- Choose people you trust, who will speak honestly and openly about you, and who are supportive of helping you find a job that fits your background, skills, and experience.
- Print your reference list on the same paper as your resume so it will match in style and quality.
- If at all possible, keep the length to one page.

DON'T:

- Include your references within your resume or the statement, "References Available Upon Request." Always create a separate document, even when submitting electronic documents online. Hiring managers and HR personnel will ask you for your references if you are one of the final candidates being considered.
- Forget to include your own contact information, preferably at the top of your reference list and in the same format and style as on your resume.
- Provide your reference list until you are specifically requested for it as part of the final interview process.
- Include anyone on your list who hasn't given you his or her permission.

The last DON'T is very important. I once answered a telephone call on my mobile phone at 4:30am (I'm in the Pacific time zone in the U.S.). Yawning and trying to force myself awake while I listened to the person speaking, I realized it was an HR person from a company on the East Coast (where it was 7:30am). He was calling me because I had been included on someone's reference list.

The bad news? This person had never asked for my permission to list me as a reference. Worse yet, I had never even worked directly with him. He had been in the department physically located next to the department I ran, but we hadn't said more than a casual "hello." I had no knowledge of this person's background, work experience, skills, or accomplishments, and the last time I'd seen the person was more than five years ago. I could not imagine why he had included me on his list of references.

As the person being called to act as a reference, I felt awful for having to tell the HR person, *"No, I cannot provide a reference for this person,"* because the next question was, *"Why not?"* Never put someone in the position of having to decline being a reference to a hiring manager or to HR personnel. Doing so will cause you to lose respect from the potential reference person, and, it might also cost you the job opportunity.

Get the most out of your references

An important part of using references is making sure you keep everyone on your list updated on your progress. Send each reference your latest resume. Then, give references a "heads up" when you've obtained an interview. Tell them about the job opportunity and the key job requirements, and forewarn them in case the hiring manager or someone from HR calls them after your interview.

Several of my clients wrongly assumed the hiring process would take a long time. They were shocked to find out that many of their references had already been contacted by the time they got home from their interview (before they had warned them about a possible phone call). Oops! Don't let this happen to you.

If you believe there is a good chance your references will be contacted after an interview, call each person to discuss any important topics that came up. For example, let's say the hiring manager stressed during the interview that she is specifically looking for someone with strong project management skills who proactively seeks out process improvement opportunities.

To increase your chances of obtaining that job, contact your references to let them know what was discussed and to ask them to specifically highlight examples of your project management accomplishments and your proactive process improvement efforts. Keeping your references "in the loop" on your job search progress will help ensure they are ready to provide you with a positive recommendation when the time comes.

A side note – electronic titling of your list of references

Finally, don't forget to carefully title the electronic document of your list of references. In Chapter 8, I provided my recommendation of titling your electronic resume document with your name, the job title, company, and date you apply (using the international date format). Follow this same format when it comes to titling your list of references. Using this format, your reference list title would be: Jane Doe Reference List_MarCom Mgr_Acme, Inc_15Sept2014. This electronic document titling format will make it easier for you to keep track of all versions of your reference list, since you might include different reference people for different job opportunities.

And a quick reminder… always carefully follow the instructions when you apply online. As I said when we discussed uploading your resume online, you might be required to upload your list of references as a PDF or as a Word document. Choose the format you're asked to use. If no format is specified, convert your list of references into a PDF document and then open the PDF to double-check it before you upload.

Use the **Reference List Example (page 268)** template in the (and online) at the back of this book to help you create your reference list.

CHAPTER 10
KEY TAKEAWAYS

A little up front preparation with your references can help differentiate you from other candidates. It may even make the difference that will sway the hiring manager to choose you for the job over all the other candidates – so take advantage of every opportunity to demonstrate your unique qualities.

CHAPTER 11

OBTAIN RECOMMENDATIONS

"Are you serious?" my 22-year-old client Brittany said, and then rolled her eyes. *"You're going to make me ask people to write recommendation letters? I thought that was something people only did back in the old days."*

Sigh. While I'd like to think I'm not as old as the dinosaurs, there are some days I definitely feel like it. Especially when it comes to discussing the topic of job recommendations with my younger clients. Brittany did have a point, though. The use of recommendation letters has changed over the last decade. In the past, obtaining recommendation letters was a requirement of the job search process. Today, not as much. Now, this step is considered optional, but savvy job seekers understand that it can help give them an edge when it comes to obtaining a position.

Today, there are two main types of recommendations: formal letters, and the recommendations you can obtain using social media tools, such as LinkedIn. A recommendation is a statement of support from someone who knows you well and with whom you've had a business relationship, such as former bosses, coworkers, direct reports, clients or customers, or even vendors. Recommendations provide additional evidence of your skills and character based on observed behaviors that will, hopefully, help the hiring manager gain a better picture of who you are and your potential to succeed in the job.

Nearly all the recruiters I've ever spoken with tell me they look for recommendations that provide a variety of perspectives on the job candidate. Specifically, they like to see at least one recommendation from a former manager, one from a coworker, and one from a direct report (if you're a supervisor or manager). As a hiring manager, I agree. I look for candidates who provide recommendations from a variety of sources (different people at different levels and at different companies or organizations), because it gives me a better overall picture of the candidate.

Formal letters of recommendation

First, let's look at formal recommendation letters. Yep, they're just like they sound – letters printed out on paper and signed by the individual making the recommendation. You'll find the requirement for providing letters of recommendation varies by company. In the past, many companies required that two letters of recommendation be submitted when you applied for the job. Now, recommendation letters have mostly become an optional item and they're generally not provided to the hiring manager until the end of an in-person job interview.

Recommendation letters tend to be a bit longer in length than the LinkedIn recommendations, but both contain much of the same information. The elements a letter of recommendation should include are:

- The date
- The hiring manager's name, title, company name and address information (if you are using the letter for a specific job opportunity and know to whom the letter should be sent; otherwise, you may ask the person to address the letter "To whom it may concern" or "Dear Hiring Manager")
- Your full name in the body of the recommendation
- The length of time the person writing the letter has known you
- The capacity in which the person writing the letter has known you (former boss, coworker, etc.)
- The key qualities or strengths that set you apart or differentiate you from others who might be applying for the same position, providing specific examples
- Any other qualifications as to why the recommender believes you would be the best person for the position, such as your education, work experience, etc.
- The recommender's name, signature, and contact information at the bottom of the letter

In the **Appendix** section of this book, see the **Recommendation Letter 1 (page 269), Recommendation Letter 2 (page 270),** and **Recommendation Letter 3 (page 271)** as examples.

After reviewing the example recommendation letters, Brittany began to understand how she could use recommendations to differentiate herself from other job seekers. Our next step was to identify people she could ask to write these, so she could have them ready to use when she began applying for positions and going on job interviews. Brittany's goal was to obtain three to five letters of recommendation.

How to obtain a letter of recommendation

As you work through the process of obtaining letters of recommendation, consider the following tips:

Whom to ask: Begin by contacting the people on your reference list – they know you well and can provide clear examples of your strengths and differentiators.

What to ask: When you contact each person, let them know you are job searching and ask if they would feel comfortable writing you a letter of recommendation.

If they say yes, what you need to provide:
- Give them as much information as possible about the current job opportunity (including the job description and requirements) or the types of jobs you are seeking.
- Talk about the key strengths or differentiators you would like them to highlight in their recommendation, so you'll know what they'll be writing about you before they write it.
- Offer to email them this list and an example letter, so they'll have these available when they sit down to write.
- Let the person know how soon you'll need their letter – always try to give them at least a week to write and send you their letter.
- Some people will offer to email you their draft letter for review and comments before they finalize it. If so, that's great!

Additional tips:

Be cautious if someone wants you to write the letter for them. Instead, offer to email the person a list of what you believe are your key strengths and differentiators (with specific examples) that they can review and then choose to incorporate in their own style, wording, and opinion.

- If possible, ask the person to write the letter on company letterhead.
- After receiving a letter, send the person a thank you note (either electronic or handwritten) letting them know you appreciate their help and will keep them informed of your job search progress.
- If the person is unable to write you a recommendation letter, don't get defensive. Some people may feel uncomfortable writing recommendation letters or not have enough available time. Be polite, be professional, and thank them for their time and consideration.

Be sincere in your request for help and ask your recommenders to be sincere in their comments about you. It is very easy for hiring managers and HR personnel to spot a letter of recommendation that has merely been copied out of a book of example letters. While a heartfelt and customized letter of recommendation can take a little time to create, it is worth the effort because it can be used to set you apart from other job candidates.

Using recommendations on social media

Now, let's turn our attention to social media, specifically LinkedIn. LinkedIn is a social networking website designed for business professionals. It allows you to share work and career-related information with other users, keep an online list of professional contacts, participate in work-related discussions, follow the activities of specific companies and people, and search for job opportunities.

Many younger job seekers are foregoing formal letters of recommendation and instead, asking people for recommendations they can include on their LinkedIn profile. Then, they choose the recommendations they want to show within their profile and can hide the others. Many of my clients print out their LinkedIn recommendations and provide them to the hiring manager at the end of job interviews instead of formal recommendation letters.

If you don't have a LinkedIn account, consider creating one. It's free, and a good way to network with others, follow what is happening with target companies, and get noticed by recruiters. If you are worried that it will be difficult to set up your profile, relax. It is very easy and the program will walk you through the steps.

Brittany was excited to show me that she already had three recommendations on her LinkedIn profile. *Her problem?* The recommendations were too short and didn't include specific information that would be helpful to a hiring manager or recruiter. Here were Brittany's three LinkedIn recommendations:

Recommendation 1 (coworker): "Brittany is fabulous and I really enjoyed working with her at ABC Company."

Recommendation 2 (former manager): "Brittany would be an asset to any company because she works hard and was a good worker at our company."

Recommendation 3: "I recommend Brittany to any company that wants to hire people with positive attitudes."

Eek! These recommendations don't convey any helpful information, and they're so generic they could refer to just about anyone. The best way to obtain high quality LinkedIn recommendations is to treat them similarly to formal recommendation letters.

- Contact only those people who know you well and can provide specific examples of your strengths and differentiators.
- For each person you ask to write a LinkedIn recommendation, provide them with three skills that you'd like them to discuss.
- Ask them to include: How long they've worked with you, background on how they know you, description of the three skills you asked them to discuss, and at least one specific success example.

After reviewing the job descriptions and requirements of the positions Brittany wanted, we jotted down some ideas of what each recommender could include about her skills and attributes. Then, Brittany contacted each person and discussed her ideas with him or her. All were enthusiastic about helping Brittany and offered to log into their LinkedIn profiles and update their previous recommendation. Here are the updated recommendations:

Updated Recommendation 1 (coworker): "Brittany and I worked together for two years at ABC Company when we were both Customer Service Representatives in the Call Center. During this time, I was impressed with her drive to excel at helping customers with their problems. Brittany has the ability to remain calm under pressure when dealing with upset or angry customers and uses her attention to detail to get to the bottom of issues and determine solutions. Brittany inspired me to always try to see problems clearly and from all angles. I hope that someday I'll have the opportunity to work with Brittany again."

Updated Recommendation 2 (former manager): "I hired Brittany into the role of Communications Coordinator when I was the Director of Marketing for XYZ Company. During the 18 months Brittany worked for me, she always listened very carefully to our internal clients' needs and goals and then came up with integrated communication plans that were within the client's available budget. Further, Brittany was good at identifying social media actions that would add value yet cost very little, such as holding Facebook contests and providing product content to popular bloggers to include in their articles. Brittany was a positive asset to the department and I highly recommend her for higher-level marketing and communication roles."

Updated Recommendation 3 (former internship manager): "I hired Brittany as a summer intern in the role of Business Analyst. During this two and a half month time period, Brittany was assigned to the Marketing Department and given the task of analyzing the sales promotion process and providing recommendations for process improvements. Brittany is very detail-oriented and I was impressed with her ability to dive deep into understanding the existing process and the customer's needs before she developed improvement recommendations. Brittany worked well with a variety of personality types and always completed her work on time. I greatly enjoyed the time she worked at Acme, Inc. and would be happy to hire her again in the future."

The updated LinkedIn recommendations are much more beneficial because they include Brittany's specific skills and examples of how she has used those skills to achieve success in past positions – valuable information to share with a hiring manager. Remember, the higher the quality of your recommendations, the more they will help you in your job quest.

Go above and beyond – your recommendations for others

As a hiring manager, many job candidates were surprised to find out I also read the LinkedIn recommendations *they* provided to others. I did this to analyze the quality of *their* recommendations. Were they well written? Did they explain the business relationship with the person and length of time? Did they state specific skills they saw the person perform? Did they provide at least one success story? Looking at the quality (or lack thereof) of recommendations a job candidate provided others gave me an idea of the potential quality of their work if I hired them.

To impress recruiters and hiring managers, review the recommendations you've provided to others on LinkedIn. Did you include the information you learned in this chapter? If not, make updates to improve the quality of your recommendations.

Use the following **Appendix** templates at the back of this book (and online) to help you create formal recommendation letters:

- **Recommendation Letter Example 1 (page 269)**
- **Recommendation Letter Example 2 (page 270)**
- **Recommendation Letter Example 3 (page 271)**

CHAPTER 11
KEY TAKEAWAYS

Recommendation letters are no longer a requirement in the job seeking process, but savvy candidates know that they can be used as a way to differentiate themselves from others. Be strategic in your use of recommendations: Obtain three to five formal recommendation letters and at least three LinkedIn recommendations that will enhance your professional profile.

PREPARE YOUR PORTFOLIO

"I've been receiving call backs and going to interviews, but I always seem to lose the hiring manager's interest half way through the interview," moaned my client as she flopped into the chair next to me. *"How can I hold their attention?"*

Sarah was in her mid-thirties and had worked as a graphic designer since graduating from college. She had also just finished her master's degree in communications at a prestigious local university. She had the skills, the experience, and the education, *so what was her problem?* Sarah hadn't created a work portfolio – a collection of examples that she could use to show hiring managers how her projects had benefited previous employers and clients.

Not everyone needs a portfolio of work examples for job interviews, but it can be helpful if you work in a career field where you've created tangible items and/or achieved measurable results that display your skills and expertise. This could include graphic designers, interior designers, communications specialists, marketing managers, project managers, advertising specialists, public relations specialists, social media experts, architects, painters, writers, etc.

After explaining the concept of a portfolio and providing a few examples, Sarah chose to create a simple website to showcase her work. One section of the website provided a brief background about Sarah, another included her contact information, and the other sections featured examples of client work, such as: logos, business cards, posters, banners, ads, sales promotions, web graphics, branding identities, monthly newsletter graphics, and so on. For each example, Sarah included a brief paragraph about the client's needs and a paragraph explaining the solution she provided.

After creating the website, Sarah updated her resume and LinkedIn profile, adding the URL so prospective employers could view her online portfolio. She also began including the URL in her customized cover letters and adding a second "teaser" page that showed the best eight items she'd created. Then Sarah printed out a selection of the projects (in full color) and put them into clear protective covers that she clipped into a three-ring binder to take with her to job interviews.

In preparation for interviews, I helped Sarah practice explaining examples by briefly sharing the customers' needs and how the solutions she created benefitted them. This gave Sarah the boost of confidence she needed, and *she never lost the attention of a hiring manager again.* She actually ended up receiving three different job offers – a nice problem to have!

"What if I don't work in a creative field?"

To benefit from a portfolio, you don't need to work in a job that is typically considered "creative" like Sarah's. Take Rosemary, for example. Rosemary was 29 years old and had just moved to Seattle with her husband from the East Coast. While still on the East Coast, Rosemary had worked her way up in the hotel hospitality industry for eight years, serving first as a swimming pool attendant, then pool concierge, front desk agent, guest concierge, front desk manager, and then into a corporate sales role.

Rosemary loved her previous sales job on the East Coast, working with current and potential corporate clients to book events such as national sales meetings, regional training sessions, and trade shows. She wanted to find a similar job in the Seattle area, but knew competition would be tough.

During the course of Rosemary's career, she had earned several hotel certifications, won four service awards, and always exceeded her quarterly and annual sales targets – she even won the highest sales award at her company. In addition, Rosemary had been recognized numerous times by customers through letters to the hotel manager, praising Rosemary for her helpful attitude and her efforts of going above and beyond the call of duty to ensure their event ran smoothly.

We decided that creating a portfolio featuring these accomplishments and accolades would be a great way to help Rosemary stand out from other job candidates. We put all of them in individual, clear protective covers and clipped them into a simple three-ring binder.

For Rosemary's portfolio, we paid careful attention to the ordering of her documents. We put the customer letters at the front of the binder and chose an important letter as the first one to highlight. It was from a very grateful company vice president. In it, he specifically praised Rosemary for her fluency in Spanish and thanked her for all the help she provided as an interpreter with their South American sales personnel at a global sales meeting the company held at the hotel. Rosemary was fluent in both English and Spanish, and this letter provided wonderful proof as to how this skill could benefit customers – much more valuable than just listing bilingual on your resume!

"How else could I use a portfolio of work to showcase my skills and expertise during interviews?"

If you've ever written marketing plans, communications plans, public relations plans, or strategic plans, you could include examples of them in your portfolio. These can be helpful tools to prove your level of expertise – just make sure you don't include any confidential company information!

If you're a business analyst or business intelligence analyst, you could provide examples of the results from some of your analysis or research projects. The key is to be able to briefly explain the background of the research or analysis, what you found out, and then how you turned the data into usable information for the company.

If you're a project manager, you could include in your portfolio of work some project initiation documents, project charters, or the work breakdown structures for important projects you've led. Just be sure you can speak to why the project was implemented (the problem) and demonstrate the results you were able to achieve.

If you're a process improvement engineer, create a portfolio that includes examples of processes you've improved. Include the before and after results, such as defect reductions, increased efficiencies, cost reductions, or revenue improvement.

Using a portfolio with work examples also makes it easier during the job interview if you're prone to forget what you wanted to say. If this happens, just flip to one of your examples and when it jogs your memory about something you did, you'll be able to quickly and easily discuss it with the hiring manager. The key is to use your portfolio as a way to jog your memory about examples you can discuss during your job interview – DON'T use it as a "crutch," where you read out loud everything you wrote in your portfolio.

"Is there anything I shouldn't include in my portfolio?"

An important consideration when creating a portfolio of work examples is to make sure you don't accidentally include any confidential company information. This is especially important if you plan to include strategic plans or marketing plans. In those cases, review what information you want to include and delete all confidential information.

This should also go without saying, but I'm going to state it here anyway: Don't include anything that might make a hiring manager feel uncomfortable. You might have done graphic design work for a company's summer 'Itsy Bitsy, Teeny Weeny Polka Dot Bikini" swimsuit line, but you might need to skip those pictures and show the winter coat collection advertisements you created instead. When in doubt, always go the more conservative route with the examples you include in your portfolio so you won't accidentally offend a recruiter or hiring manager.

CHAPTER 12
KEY TAKEAWAYS   A portfolio is a collection of work examples that you can share during interviews to demonstrate and prove your skills and expertise. Creating a portfolio isn't always required, but it can be a great way to differentiate yourself from other candidates.

PART 4

POLISH YOUR
PERSONAL BRAND

POLISH YOUR LINKEDIN PROFILE

Recruiters and managers aren't hiding from the growth and popularity of social media. In fact, they're using tools like LinkedIn as a pre-interview tactic to narrow down candidates. LinkedIn is a great tool for job seekers. As I mentioned earlier in the book, it offers exposure by making an electronic version of your resume viewable by recruiters, hiring managers, and HR professionals.

Screening a LinkedIn profile is similar to screening a resume. Most recruiters and HR personnel will initially spend about 30 seconds looking at it. If your profile doesn't entice them to keep reading, they'll move on to the next one. To ensure this doesn't happen to you, here is advice on what hiring managers, HR personnel, and recruiters are looking for when scanning a LinkedIn profile:

Headline: Don't try to be overly cute. If you're looking for a job, be specific and concise, such as "Experienced graphic designer looking to work at an entrepreneurial start-up."

Picture: Don't skip posting a picture, but use a professional one that is appropriate for your desired job/industry. Avoid using pictures where you're at a party with drink in hand or in revealing clothing, and don't use a picture where you've cut out the people standing next to you.

Background Summary: Because job candidates have so little time to catch a reviewer's attention, the Background Summary is critical. Write a thorough summary that provides key details about your professional experience, including the most important characteristics that you're trying to market or sell to prospective employers.

Additional Info/Advice for Contacting: Provide information on how recruiters may contact you and what you wish to be contacted for (such as job opportunities, speaking engagements, consulting work, organizational training opportunities, etc.) Move your contact information up so it is located within your profile in the area just underneath your Background Summary – you want to make it as easy as possible for a potential employer to contact you!

Experience: In this section, you should tell your work "story." Use the information from your new or updated resume to clearly present your work experience and how you've progressed through your career. When looking for potential or passive candidates on LinkedIn, most recruiters search for relevant experience compared to their open positions, so use keywords that are typical for your industry/job and use job titles that are easy to understand.

Education: Include your college degrees along with any continuing education. If your grade point average was high, include it. You can add your certifications in this section or in a separate "Certifications" section.

Recommendations: As discussed in Chapter 11, you should have at least three well-written LinkedIn recommendations that support your skills, areas of expertise, and work experience. Recruiters look for recommendations from a variety of sources, so make sure to include recommendations from former bosses, coworkers, direct reports, clients or customers, and vendors.

There are other sections within a LinkedIn profile, but these are the most important areas to focus on when you're looking for a job. Additionally, if you have examples of previous work, you may want to include those as proof of your skills or expertise. Simply upload the pictures or documents into the appropriate section within your profile. You can also include any work-related awards, publications you've written, or job-related volunteer experience. A final tip – take advantage of the LinkedIn function that allows you to create a customized URL link that includes your first and last name.

What do recruiters NOT care about?

Ask any recruiter and they'll tell you they don't care much about the "Organizations" section and endorsements for "Skills & Expertise." Most recruiters I've spoken with recognize anyone can endorse you for any skill, which doesn't offer them much value in the recruiting process. Don't waste time soliciting skill endorsements. Instead, focus on obtaining high-quality recommendations from a variety of people who know you well.

For potential employers, the biggest turn-offs in a candidate's LinkedIn profile are:

- An incomplete job history
- Experience that doesn't include specific accomplishments in each position
- Poor grammar
- Spelling errors
- Bad or inappropriate profile pictures

Just like a poorly written resume or cover letter, these attributes create the perception that an individual is lazy, doesn't care, could be hiding something, or lacks professionalism – not a good way to start off a relationship with a recruiter or hiring manager!

What information can potential employers gain through social media?

With the growth of social media, employers have access to more information about you than ever before. Because of this, you should expect NO privacy regarding information you share publicly. Any information you post online becomes fair game for employers to review. It doesn't mean they *will* look at it, but it *does* mean you should always think carefully about anything you post, anywhere on the Internet. Knowing this, force yourself to display the most professional online image possible.

Given the vast amount of information employers can gather online, there are some boundaries they legally should not cross. There have been issues of recruiters and hiring managers asking job candidates for social media passwords or to log onto social media accounts so they can look over their shoulder at personal content. Employers should NEVER do this. There are U.S. privacy laws that serve to protect private information and many states have also taken this a step further by passing legislation that prevents employers, schools, or both from demanding access to or asking for passwords to social media accounts.

Companies *should* proactively train HR personnel and hiring managers on the applicable state and federal laws as well as the do's and don'ts when it comes to using social media in the hiring process. However, you should be prepared, just in case you find yourself being interviewed by someone who isn't properly trained.

What if you find yourself in this situation? First, be mindful of keeping your business and personal profiles separate. For example, use LinkedIn for professional purposes only and keep your Facebook account limited to close friends and family (NOT coworkers), carefully controlling your privacy settings. This way if an interviewer asks you to accept a "friend request" on Facebook to see your information, you can politely respond that you keep your Facebook profile limited to only family and close friends, but that they may connect with you on LinkedIn and access your business information there.

If an interviewer asks for your social media password (which should rarely, if ever, occur), deflect their question by saying something such as: *"Is there something in particular you're looking for that wasn't on my resume? If so, please feel free to review my professional profile on LinkedIn, or, I'd be happy to discuss anything that relates to my qualifications for this job and my employment history with you while I'm here."*

There will always be a few fringe people who cross ethical and legal boundaries during the hiring process, such as asking for a social media password, but these incidences should be rare. If it happens to you, be prepared with a response. Then stop and ask yourself, *"Is this really a company (or manager) I'd want to work for?"*

CHAPTER 13
KEY TAKEAWAYS

The use of social media (such as LinkedIn) in the hiring process continues to grow. Recruiters and hiring managers aren't hiding from technology tools, and neither should you. Because social media gives employers access to more information on job candidates, be smart and strategic in how you participate. Take advantage of social media by presenting a profile that depicts the type of employee a company would want to hire.

CONDUCT PERSONAL BRANDING

Companies spend a lot of money and expend a lot of effort to build their brands. Why is building a brand so important? Because it is a way for companies to stand out, helping a prospective customer or client remember their product. For example, when you hear someone say the words "Coca-Cola," what do you picture? The makers of Coca-Cola hope you remember not just the brand's name, but also the unique shape of their original glass bottle, the color and shape of the logo, and the refreshing and bubbly taste of their product.

Do other brands stand out in your mind? Because I'm from Seattle, Nordstrom immediately pops into my mind. For me, Nordstrom stands for high-quality shoes and clothing that I purchase in person, so I can receive their unique level of customer service. When I think about Zappos, I think of shoes and other items I can quickly and easily purchase online.

Companies use branding to help differentiate their products in the minds of customers. So if you *think of yourself as a product and your career as a business,* then personal branding efforts will help you stand out to recruiters, hiring managers, higher-level management, even industry experts or those looking for experts. And if done correctly, personal brand building can positively impact your career and your job search efforts.

Developing a *personal* brand is similar to product branding. The overall goal is to differentiate yourself (the product) in the market so you can attain your objectives, such as landing your dream job or a promotion. The process includes defining your brand attributes, positioning your brand in a different way than your competitors, and then managing all aspects of your personal brand.

How to start building your personal brand

The biggest issue I see when it comes to personal branding is a lack of adequate research and strategizing. There's an old saying, "Ready, aim, fire," but when it comes to personal branding, many people work backwards with "Fire, ready, aim." People tend to get so excited about starting, that they forget to do their homework before taking action.

Lauren is a good example of this. When she hired me as her career coach, Lauren was in her late twenties, had a college degree in business, and had earned certifications in Six Sigma process improvement, Lean, and project management. *Her problem?* She had been working in positions that had nothing to do with her dream job – leading large, cross-functional project teams for a Fortune 500 corporation. The right people weren't seeing her skills and Lauren felt frustrated with her career progress, or lack thereof.

Lauren needed a way to stand out so management would see her expertise. I focused our sessions on teaching Lauren the steps for developing her personal brand:

Step 1: Define your overall aspirations. Be specific and clearly define your goals and objectives. Is it to become known as the best project manager in your company? Obtain a sales position in the medical equipment industry? Move from a job in marketing to a job in strategic planning or business development? Carefully think about what you want and define your career ambitions.

Step 2: Conduct research. How are those who have made it to where you want to be conducting their personal branding efforts? What can you learn from what others are doing, be their efforts good or bad? Who are your biggest competitors and what are they doing to brand themselves?

Step 3: Determine your brand attributes. What do you want your personal brand to convey? What adjectives do you want people to associate with you (as the product) and why? In what niche of the market do you want to become known?

Step 4: Assess your current state. How do people currently perceive you? Take the time to speak with many different people to understand how they view your strengths and then use this information as you create your personal brand. How large is the gap between the current you and the person you want others to perceive you to be? What needs to change and why?

Step 5: Create your game plan. Your game plan should include more than just branding yourself in social media. Your plan needs to include all aspects of you, as a product. Defining your plan should take into account the tangible and intangible characteristics of personal branding, such as attire, hair, makeup, behavior, verbal and non-verbal communication. Your plan should also include the specific social media aspects you'll use to convey your new personal brand, such as business networking sites (like LinkedIn), social networking sites (such as Facebook), Twitter, blogs, etc. It should also include other types of personal marketing, such as speaking events at industry meetings, joining and interacting at association events, even providing free training sessions in your area of expertise.

Step 6: Manage your brand. Proactively manage all aspects of your brand, ensuring these aspects are in sync and that they continue to reinforce your brand attributes and market niche. For example, your LinkedIn picture should look similar to the in-person you, your tweets (on Twitter) and any social media posts should stay within your market niche, and your in-person behavior should be representative of how you want others to perceive you. So if you've branded yourself in social media as a creative fashion diva, then make sure that extends to how you come across in person (attire, hair, makeup, jewelry, etc.).

Personal branding isn't simple, but forcing yourself to think through your unique strengths, your career goals and aspirations, and how you want others to perceive you can have dramatically positive results. And sometimes, the most difficult things in life are those that help us the most.

In Lauren's case, we first needed to clean up her online persona. This included updating her LinkedIn profile to make it current and much more professional, removing pictures on Facebook that could cause potential problems (such as pictures of Lauren at wild parties drinking alcohol and smoking), and removing all past tweets that did not relate to her area of expertise.

Lauren's personal branding game plan also included:

- Writing a series of guest blogs for several websites on the topics of process improvement and project management to increase the amount of information that came up when someone searched for her name online.
- Tweeting and posting on LinkedIn five times per week on topics related to her expertise, including tips, comments, and links to helpful articles and blogs.
- Providing free lunch training sessions to local business associations on the topic of project management for beginners.
- Keywording both her resume and her LinkedIn profile to ensure they included all the appropriate industry words that relate to process improvement, project management, Lean, and Six Sigma.
- Joining relevant groups on LinkedIn and participating in discussions related to her areas of expertise.
- Becoming a member of several associations related to her areas of expertise.
- Looking for process improvement opportunities within her current department and volunteering to lead project teams to reengineer processes.
- Working actively to expand her LinkedIn network.

It took about nine months of branding work until Lauren began receiving inquiries from recruiters through her LinkedIn account. Her in-person networking efforts at association meetings and volunteer speaking events also helped Lauren build her personal brand. In turn, this generated interest from hiring managers, who began asking her for her resume at various local events. Within a year, Lauren accepted a project manager position at a company with great potential for her future career advancement.

As you work through your personal branding efforts, consider all of the various tools you could use to convey your brand. Some examples include:

- Your business cards
- Your resume
- Customized cover letters
- Portfolio of your work (online or hard copy)

- Social media profiles and posts, such as LinkedIn, Twitter, Facebook, or Instagram
- Your own website
- Writing your own blog or guest blogs for other websites
- Your overall image: hairstyle, attire, makeup, jewelry, and behavior/communication
- Providing free training sessions on your area of expertise
- Becoming a member of various business associations and using them to network
- Joining online groups and participating in discussions that are linked to your areas of expertise

Create a professional online image

As part of developing your game plan for personal branding, here are tips for developing your professional online image.

Think of social media profiles like megaphones. Never post anything online that you'd be embarrassed to see on the front page of a newspaper. Facebook and Twitter shouldn't be forums to vent about everything you hate in life or in your job. Employers can see more than you think.

Google yourself. Regularly search your name online and evaluate if the results represent you in a professional manner. If not, take actions to clean up your online image. Creating a blog or Twitter account can help bury the search results you'd like to hide (the results you can't remove through your own efforts). In addition, set up a search engine alert for your name – these email you every time a new mention of your name appears online. You can set these up on almost any search engine, such as Google, Bing, Yahoo, etc.

Do a deep clean. Go through your social media profiles and delete anything inappropriate before sending out resumes. Also, the privacy/security settings for social networking sites change frequently, so double-check to ensure they're at your preferred level.

Use LinkedIn. As we discussed in the previous chapter, LinkedIn is a great tool for job seekers. It offers exposure by making an electronic version of your resume viewable by recruiters, hiring managers, and HR professionals. With this in mind, always keep your profile updated with your current job title, responsibilities and accomplishments, awards, and a recent picture.

Actively search for networking opportunities. Social media sites lend many opportunities to make connections with others in your field, potential clients, or your next employer. It is easy to seek out like-minded professionals on Twitter and LinkedIn. And as always, if you decide to take your networking offline, meet in a public place.

Position yourself as an expert. Social media allows you to get your name out there by demonstrating your talent and setting you apart in your job search. Consider writing a blog focused on your area of expertise or participate in online communities and discussion groups.

Manage your image. Your pictures on social media will often be the first time a person actually sees you. Create the perception you want by having professional portrait pictures taken for use in social media. If you don't have professional-looking photographs, people may assume you don't take your career seriously or that you are immature.

A final note of caution

Now that you understand the various ways you can brand yourself using social media, I'd like to leave you with a note of caution: *Use social media wisely.* What you post or tweet could cost you that much-coveted job or promotion, if you're not careful.

Many people forget that what they post on social networking sites can be viewed by many people, including recruiters and hiring managers. And if you're trying to obtain a job or get a promotion at work, what you write could have an impact on whether or not you get that job.

Let's say you post on Facebook or tweet about how awful your current manager is, how bored you are with your job, or how irritated you are with some of your customers' requests. You may think they're just innocent comments written "in the heat of the moment," but if you're a manager, would you want to hire or promote someone who criticizes their manager or isn't customer focused? Doubtful.

What you share could have an incredibly negative impact on getting your next job or promotion (or even keeping your existing job). So before you air your dirty laundry on social media, before you blog about your sexual escapades, and before you throw insults at your ex via Twitter, take a deep breath and think twice before pressing the "post" button.

CHAPTER 14 KEY TAKEAWAYS To differentiate yourself from other job seekers, don't just build a career; build your personal brand. Developing a personal brand is similar to product branding. The overall goal with branding is to differentiate yourself (the product) in the market so you can attain your objectives, be those landing your dream job or a promotion.

PART 5

SCORE AN INTERVIEW

CHAPTER 15

OBTAIN HELP FROM INTERNAL SPONSORS AND COACHES

Stephanie felt like she had been doing everything right when it came to obtaining a job. Yet she wasn't getting call backs to come in for an interview. *Her problem?* She was seeking jobs within a highly competitive industry, but wasn't using sponsors or internal coaches to get her foot in the door.

How about you? Are you still not obtaining that coveted job, even though you've been doing all the right prep work? If there's a position you *really want* or a company you *have to* work for, maybe it's time to find an *internal sponsor* and/or *coach*. These are company insiders who can provide tips about the company, potential positions, the associated hiring managers, even internal politics and the cultural environment. They can also serve as your personal advocates or references as you compete for jobs within the company.

An internal *sponsor* is someone who works at the company, provides you with background information, and answers your questions. They will also step up and vouch for you and your abilities and speak with the hiring manager and the assigned HR recruiter on your behalf. Use an internal sponsor to proactively open doors to a job, introduce you to hiring managers, or to help with your career advancement.

An internal *coach* is someone who provides you with the information you need, but maybe doesn't know you well enough to agree to recommend you or doesn't know the hiring manager well enough to speak to them about you (or just aren't comfortable doing so). Use an internal coach to guide you through the company hiring process and to help you avoid pitfalls.

How can you find an internal sponsor or coach? Spread the word through your existing network that you're looking for someone who works at XYZ company. If no one knows of someone, you may need to conduct some new networking activities, such as attending local business association meetings or contacting your local chamber of commerce for upcoming events. Create a list of all the networking functions you can attend to meet someone who works at XYZ company.

What this typically comes down to is the old "friend of a friend" situation - finding a person who knows someone working where you'd like to work. For example, Stephanie began networking intensively to find an internal sponsor or coach. When she attended a local women's association event, she happened to run into a friend from high school. Her high school friend introduced her to someone else at the networking event who happened to have a sister who worked at Stephanie's target company. See how this works?

Your mission, should you choose to accept it, is to find at least one internal sponsor or coach who will help you obtain entrance into your desired company.

They exchanged business cards and the next day Stephanie emailed the woman a quick note, letting her know how much she enjoyed meeting her at the networking event and that she looked forward to meeting her sister to discuss her employer. Later that day when she checked email, she had already received a response. Even better, the response email was copied to the woman's sister and included all her contact information. Stephanie called the sister and they arranged to meet for coffee later that week. *The result?* The woman became Stephanie's coach, providing her with important information about the company, hiring manager, and department. In the end, Stephanie got the job she was seeking and also gained a great friend.

Your mission, should you choose to accept it, is to find at least one internal sponsor or coach who will help you obtain entrance into your desired company. Because they're insiders, they usually know the main players, understand the culture, the environment and the politics and, hopefully, they'll even know the hiring manager for the job you're seeking.

If you already know an insider and they're familiar with your work background, education, and skills – great! Find out if they're willing to act as your sponsor and help put in a good word about you to the hiring manager. Taking that one step further, ask if they're willing to be a reference or even write you a letter of recommendation (either a formal letter or a recommendation on LinkedIn).

If you don't know anyone inside your target company, network as much as possible to find someone who works there so you can obtain an introduction and sit down with them for a discussion. Have a list of questions ready, such as...

Questions to ask a sponsor or coach

- What is the culture and environment like at the company? Is it casual or formal?
- What do you know about the hiring manager? Their background? Their management style?
- What do you know about the department where this position resides? How many employees work in this department?
- How does the company support employee growth and training?
- Does the company promote from within?
- How long do employees tend to stay with the company?
- How diverse is the workforce? How diverse is the management team?
- Is there anything you recommend I do to prepare myself for the interview?

Expanding your network to find sponsors and coaches requires some proactive work. The good news is that there are an almost unlimited number of places to network. Here are a few ideas to help you begin your networking efforts...

How to network

- Attend local women's, business, and professional association meetings.
- Attend your city's chamber of commerce meetings and networking events.
- Join the alumni association at your college or university and seek out networking events.
- Join networking groups (such as eWomenNetwork).

- Join online networking sites (such as Meetup).
- Join applicable groups on LinkedIn and then look for networking events.
- Research networking events happening near you (try Eventbrite, NetParty, FindNetworkingEvents, or job-hunt).
- Check with your local library for job networking events.
- Check with your church for networking events.
- Join Toastmasters and learn new skills while you network.

As you start attending networking events, keep in mind your objective: To find internal sponsors and coaches. Also, remember that you can't just show up at an event, you have to actively circulate throughout the attendees, striking up conversations. Here are a few things to think about when it comes to attending networking events...

Networking tips

- Yes, it's a social event, but treat it as a business event. Always act professionally and don't drink too much alcohol, if it is offered.
- Arrive on time. Better yet, arrive early.
- Dress appropriately. If you're unsure, dress in business attire (a suit) as it is best to err on the side of being too conservative.
- Prepare what you will discuss. Know how you'll introduce yourself to others and how you'll explain the help you're seeking – be brief!
- Smile, smile, smile! It will help you look approachable and open to discussion.
- Move around the event and meet people. Don't hide out in a corner talking with only a few people – push yourself.
- Bring business cards.
- Think about your main objective, but don't come across as pushy.
- Be a good listener – don't just focus on your own agenda.

You'll likely speak with a lot of people in your quest to find internal sponsors and coaches; so don't take a "No" personally. Everyone is busy and they might be swamped with other things and unable to help. Don't get discouraged or take a "No" to heart, because it is probably not about you but about their lack of time.

No matter what happens, remain professional. Whether or not you obtain the job you're seeking, don't forget to thank your sponsors and/or coaches for their help. At a minimum, send them a handwritten thank you note. Better yet, send them the thank you note *and* take them to lunch. Remember, even if it didn't work out for this specific job, they still might be able to help you in the future. So treat them kindly, appreciatively, and with the utmost of respect – you just might gain yourself a career advocate.

CHAPTER 15
KEY TAKEAWAYS

If you're still not obtaining that coveted job, even though you've been doing all the right prep work, consider finding internal sponsors and coaches. These are company insiders who can help you proactively open doors to a new job, help with your career advancement, and guide you through the company's hiring process - helping you avoid pitfalls.

CHAPTER 16

WRITE CUSTOMIZED COVER LETTERS

My client, Stephanie (mentioned in the previous chapter) crinkled her nose and grimaced. *"Yuck, that's the part I hate the most when it comes to applying for jobs."* Her comment made me smile. *"I mean, why should I even bother writing cover letters? Most hiring managers don't even read them, do they?"* she added.

Stephanie had a point... hiring managers *do* pay more attention to resumes than cover letters. And while a cover letter likely won't be what lands you the job, it can be what knocks you out of the running to receive a call back for an interview. Stephanie was a good example of this. She had an excellent resume with solid experience as a call center manager, but she couldn't figure out why she wasn't getting more job interviews. *The problem?* Stephanie had been using generic, template cover letters. She wasn't customizing them to fit each job opportunity.

Using pre-written cover letters is never a good idea. When you receive a letter addressed to "Dear Sir/Madam" or "To whom it may concern," does it feel special? No! The same goes for a hiring manger. Don't let your cover letters be seen as workplace junk mail. Take the time to customize and use them as an opportunity to sell yourself.

How can you do this? Use the information you uncovered during your company and industry research efforts (Chapter 5) and your discussions with your internal sponsors and coaches (Chapter 15). *Here is an example:* Remember all of Stephanie's networking efforts that we discussed in the last chapter? Through networking events, Stephanie found someone who worked at her target company and was willing to act as an inside coach. Over lunch one day, this coach provided Stephanie with a lot of valuable information. She told Stephanie that the company was currently experiencing high turnover in their call center and having difficulty training new employees. Stephanie also found out the company planned to convert to a different IT platform later in the year – the same software program she had used at a previous company.

Toward the end of their lunch conversation, Stephanie's coach lowered her voice to a whisper and leaned in to say, *"Maybe I shouldn't be telling you this, but I'm personal friends with Carrie, the hiring manager. She mentioned to me this week that the candidates she interviewed for the Call Center Manager position seemed young and inexperienced compared with what she was looking to hire."* The coach also told her about an upcoming Chamber of Commerce networking event that the hiring manager was planning to attend.

This was *exactly* the kind of information Stephanie needed to create a customized cover letter that differentiated her from other job seekers. Here's what I mean:

Company issue #1: High turnover and difficulty training all the new hires. **Solution:** Stephanie had many years of experience in new hire training and was responsible for this in her previous positions.

Company issue #2: Switching to a new IT platform later this year and expecting the conversion process to be difficult. **Solution:** Stephanie not only had experience with the new software system, but in a previous position she helped management test the software. She also wrote the internal training manuals and trained all the call center employees on how to use the new software program.

Company issue #3: Hiring manager is looking for someone who is professionally mature and has experience working in a call center environment and is having difficulty finding such a candidate. **Solution:** Stephanie had nine years of experience working in call centers, working her way up from entry level to management positions. This work experience should make Stephanie highly qualified and very valuable in the position.

Because of the help Stephanie received from her coach, she also received the full name and title of the hiring manager so she could include it in her cover letter (avoid "Dear Sir or Madam" if possible). Along with this, Stephanie gained a valuable internal reference. Using all of this information, I worked with Stephanie to create a customized cover letter to the hiring manager. Go check out the letter we created in the **Customized Cover Letter Example (page 272)** in the **Appendix** of this book.

Stephanie's customized cover letter (in the Appendix) is a great example of the kind of cover letters that will help to distinguish yourself from other candidates and help you advance forward in the hiring process. Your customized cover letter should contain the following elements:

Header: The date, company name, address, the name and title of the hiring manager (if you know this information)

Salutation: The name of the hiring manager (if you don't know his/her name, you could use "Dear Hiring Manager)

First paragraph: An opening paragraph referencing the job and job ID# of the position you're seeking, how you found out about the position (if relevant) and/or the person who referred you

Middle paragraph(s): A paragraph or two that briefly explains why you believe you are the best person for the job (choose no more than three reasons to highlight in this paragraph)

Closing paragraph: A paragraph that establishes the next steps for contact (personally, I never call or follow up on a Monday morning or on a Friday afternoon, as these times tend to be very hectic for hiring managers)

Sign-off: Your name, signature, and contact information - contact information may be listed at the top of the letter, in the last paragraph, or underneath your signature

As you create your customized cover letters, here are a few additional tips:

- Use the same style, layout, and font as your resume.
- Don't write a novel – try to be as concise as possible.
- If you print a hard copy, use the same paper you used to print your resume (so it will match in style and quality).
- If the job application requires you to upload your cover letter, save it into a PDF format before uploading or emailing it – unless the instructions say otherwise.

Additionally, just like your resume, your cover letters should be free of spelling and grammar errors. As a hiring manager, I have come across many letters with multiple misspelled words, grammar mistakes, and unfinished sentences. But one particular faux pas stands out in my mind.

The open position was for a Communications Manager within a large marketing department that I led. The candidate's cover letter seemed very stale and lackluster. Sure enough, when I typed a few of the sentences from the letter into an online search engine, it came up as a pre-written example that had been posted online about ten years prior. Worse yet, the candidate made several spelling errors, was missing a few words, and forgot to include his contact information anywhere on the document.

> A well-written cover letter won't necessarily land you the job. But a poorly written letter can eliminate your chances of getting hired.

As I mentioned at the beginning of this chapter, a well-written cover letter won't necessarily land you the job. But a poorly written letter can eliminate your chances of getting hired. To me, a cover letter provides a first look at the job candidate's communication skills. Clearly, the candidate's cover letter I just described didn't leave a good impression. The job required excellent written communication skills and innovation/creativity, and his use of a standardized pre-written form letter with multiple errors gave me no indication he had those skills.

Stephanie, on the other hand, submitted her application, resume and customized cover letter online. When she attended the Chamber of Commerce networking event she had mentioned in her cover letter, she was able to meet Carrie Apple, the hiring manager. She and Carrie had a great discussion and Stephanie was able to convey her interest in the position, her targeted experience, and her passion for working in call centers.

Stephanie also brought a hard copy of her resume and cover letter with her, which she gave to Carrie at the end of their conversation. Her actions prompted the hiring manager to schedule Stephanie for an interview the very next day! To make a long story short, Stephanie was offered the job right after the interview – and she accepted!

See how everything is starting to come together and the importance of networking and being prepared to sell yourself for a job opportunity? The prep work we did early on, like researching a company, analyzing your strengths and weaknesses, and networking really pays off when you find yourself face-to-face with a hiring manager, whether it is during an interview or at a networking event.

There is an old saying that, "You will never have a second chance to make a first impression" – attributed variably to Oscar Wilde, Will Rogers, or even Mark Twain. Your cover letter is the perfect opportunity to make an excellent first impression and set yourself apart from other job candidates, so take the time to write a really good one.

A side note – electronic titling of your cover letters

I discussed the importance of carefully titling your electronic documents in Chapter 8 (Prepare Your Resume) and in Chapter 10 (Prepare Your List of References). Continue with a consistent formatting technique when it comes to your customized cover letters. Use your name, the job title, company, and date you apply (using the international date format). To keep the document title from being too long, abbreviate where possible. As an example, if your name is Jane Doe and you're applying for the position of Marketing Communications Manager at a company named Acme, Incorporated, here is how you would title your electronic cover letter document: Jane Doe Cover Letter_MarCom Mgr_Acme, Inc_15Sept2014.

This electronic document titling format will make it easy for the hiring manager or HR personnel to see whose document it is, and, it will make it easier for you to keep track of all your cover letters – since you'll be creating a customized cover letter for every job to which you apply.

Use the following **Appendix** template at the back of this book (and online) to help you create customized cover letters:

- **Customized Cover Letter Example (page 272)**

CHAPTER 16
KEY TAKEAWAYS

While a cover letter might not be what lands you the job, it can be what eliminates you from receiving a call back for an interview. Don't let your cover letters become workplace junk mail. Take the time to customize and use them as an opportunity to sell yourself to the hiring manager.

PART 6

PREP FOR
INTERVIEW SUCCESS

ANTICIPATE INTERVIEW QUESTIONS AND PREPARE ANSWERS

Taylor successfully completed all of the necessary steps to obtain her first job interview. *Her problem?* The interview was in just three days, but she wasn't sure how to prepare.

Securing your first job interview is an exciting moment. Take a little time to savor that feeling (do a happy dance) and then use your excitement and energy to help you ace it. The best way to ensure you'll have a successful interview? Preparation, preparation, preparation, so you'll be able to walk in the door filled with confidence and walk out with a job offer. All it takes is the ability to focus on completing some specific steps to make sure you'll be able to shine like a star during your job interview.

Taylor could spend countless hours or even days trying to prepare an answer for every possible interview question in the world. But no one has that kind of time, and truly, it is not necessary. An inside tip – hiring managers typically ask questions from just five categories. With this in mind, you can prepare for the questions you'll likely receive, and that's exactly how I helped Taylor.

Categories of questions for which you should prepare

To start, these are the five groups of questions you should consider when prepping for an interview:

Background questions focus on helping hiring managers gain an understanding of your work experience/history, skills, education, and qualifications for the job.

Job/Company/Industry questions test your knowledge and understanding of the position, company, and industry.

Functional Fit questions verify/validate your level of knowledge, skills, and competency on key aspects of the job.

Style/Personality questions focus on learning about your personality, social style, and work style.

Future Orientation questions help hiring managers determine your career goals and aspirations and how well you'll interact with others.

Hiring managers often begin job interviews with *background* questions so they can quickly gain insights into the candidate. Examples of background questions include:

- Walk me through each job you've held and tell me the most important thing you learned in each position.
- Tell me about your most important career accomplishment.
- What is the toughest work challenge you've ever faced and how did you handle it?
- Tell me about your last few performance appraisals. What were your evaluation results? What were you praised for and what were the suggestions for improvement?
- What have you done lately to "upgrade" yourself to improve your knowledge or skills?

Once hiring managers understand your education, work experience, and overall background, they'll usually move on to questions that test your understanding of the job, the company, and sometimes the industry. Examples of *job/company/industry* questions include:

- Tell me what you know about this open position.
- What interests you about this job? Or, Why did you apply for this job? Or, Why do you want this job?
- Looking at the job description, take me through each requirement and explain why you believe you are qualified in each of the areas listed.
- If you were the hiring manager for this job, what qualities or attributes would you look for in candidates?

- Tell me what you know about this company and industry.

Hiring managers will also spend time determining the functional fit of a candidate. With these questions, they assess a job candidate's knowledge, skills, and experience for a specific job. This part of the interview might also include assessment tests to determine how well the candidate performs in required areas, such as coding skills for IT positions, writing and editing skills for public relations jobs, or typing skills for administrative assistants. Examples of *functional fit* questions include:

- Sales job: Walk me through the most complex sale you've ever made and why you believe it was complex. Explain each step in the sales process you typically follow.
- Marketing job: What are some of the biggest issues you've encountered in product launch plans, and, how did you overcome them? What are the components you typically include in a marketing plan?
- Administrative assistant job: What have you found are the most important skills for being successful in this type of role? Walk me through your skill level in preparing presentations. Tell me about the most difficult or complex presentation you ever created.
- Database administrator job: Walk me through your process of troubleshooting problems/issues.

For a hiring manager, the functional fit questions identify those who have lied on their resume or have stretched the truth about their skills or experience. That is because the candidate will be unable to answer the more difficult questions. Keep in mind that the toughest functional fit questions will be specific to the job you applied for, so brainstorm a list of potential questions like those listed above.

Additionally, hiring managers will often ask questions to help them understand your *style, personality,* and how you think about things. Examples of these questions include:

- How would coworkers describe you?
- Tell me your approach to setting goals for yourself.
- Describe your decision-making process.
- What do you believe is the best way to handle conflict?

- What frustrates you the most?

The last of the five types of questions are those that deal with your future career goals and aspirations. Examples of *future orientation* questions include:

- What are your career goals for the next five years? Ten years?
- Tell me about some of your recent career goals and what you've done to achieve them.
- How do you evaluate whether you or others have been successful?
- Tell me about some of the items on your personal development plan.
- Why should I hire you for this job over all the other candidates who have applied?

Cultural fit interviews

Prior to an in-person interview with the hiring manager, you may be scheduled for a telephone interview by a Human Resources recruiter to screen for "cultural fit." Culture is loosely defined as the core values, behaviors, and personalities that make up an organization. These are based on the beliefs, attitudes, and priorities of its members as well as how they view their work and themselves.

The interview to assess cultural fit is important, because company cultures can vary greatly, and not every employee will do well or be happy in every culture. For example, someone who would like working for a small, start-up company might not enjoy the formality or structure of working for a large bank or global corporation. The reverse is also true – someone who enjoys the challenges of working for a large, international company with thousands of employees might not be a good fit for a small company where she interacts with the same 10-20 people every day.

The goal of the cultural fit interview is to assess job candidates' personal and social/work styles and preferences to ensure they are a good fit within the hiring organization's culture. HR reps/recruiters often conduct cultural fit interviews, but in small companies this responsibility may fall on the hiring manager. Examples of *cultural fit* questions include:

- Describe your ideal work environment.
- Explain a work environment or culture in which you would NOT be happy.

- Describe the behavior and characteristics of the best boss you've ever had.
- Tell me about your preferred work style (e.g. alone or on a team, with close supervision or allowed to work independently, fast-paced or slower paced).

Additional interview tips

Now that Taylor had an overall understanding of the types of questions she might be asked during her job interview, we focused on her answers. The most important aspect of answering any question is to listen carefully and never interrupt the interviewer. Before you respond, make sure you fully understand the question. If you don't understand something about the question, ask for clarification before you begin your answer.

Taylor had a habit of immediately replying to questions, so I reminded her that it is okay to take a few seconds to think about her answer. She also had a tendency to over-think our practice questions and then try to respond with what she thought the hiring manager would want to hear. So I encouraged Taylor to take a more personal approach in her answers by sharing true stories and examples of how she had handled situations in the past as well as her personal philosophy on the topic at hand.

What many people don't realize is that it's okay to show your personality during an interview. Companies don't want to hire robots, they want to hire real people... so relax, be yourself, and don't be afraid to let the interviewer see your personality or sense of humor. Go ahead and make that hiring manager laugh with your story of what went wrong in a project you led earlier in your career, just be sure to also explain how you were able to fix the problem and what you learned from the situation. Here are additional interview tips I reviewed with Taylor:

- Answer questions directly; don't be evasive.
- Don't lie or stretch the truth.
- Avoid beginning sentences with: "Um," "So," "Well," and "Okay."
- Don't begin answers with: "Good question" or "Now that's an interesting question" – what were all the other questions, uninteresting and boring?

- Don't refuse to answer a question, but if an interviewer asks a question that makes you feel uncomfortable or that you believe is illegal (such as "How old are you?" or "Do you plan on having any children?"), try saying something like, "Help me understand how that information would be helpful to your decision of the best candidate." And, be very polite and professional when you respond.

Prepare responses to the specific job requirements

After practicing your answers to the five categories of questions in the previous section, pull out the job posting and read it again. Look at the area within the job posting that lists the job requirements or responsibilities. Now, try turning each item into a question, and then think about how you could respond during the job interview.

For example, let's say you've applied for a position as a Marketing Communications Manager and the first job requirement states: "Develops marketing communications plans to support the sale of the company's products and services." Pretend you are the hiring manager and think about how you might turn that into a question. Such as, "Tell me about your experience writing marketing communications plans." Or, "What have you found to be the biggest obstacles when it comes to creating and implementing marketing communications plans?" Then, practice how you could answer these questions to demonstrate your qualifications for the job.

Let's look at one more example, this time for the position of Product Manager within a marketing department. If one of the job requirements/ responsibilities is to "Oversee market research, monitor competitive activity, and identify customer needs," how might you ask that as a question? A hiring manager could ask you to explain your experience conducting market research. He or she could ask you, "What are the best methods you've found to monitor competitor activity?" They might ask, "What are the biggest difficulties you've found when it comes to monitoring competitive activity?" As far as the "customer needs" component of the requirement, you might be asked to explain the process you follow to identify customer needs or to explain how you've used customer needs information to improve products and provide a few examples. Once you've written out the possible questions you could be asked, think through your responses and then write them down.

Follow this process all the way through to the last item on the job posting: Read the job requirements and responsibilities, brainstorm potential questions, and then determine your answers. Once you're able to explain your background, skills, or experience for each requirement listed, you are more likely to do well in the interview.

The S.T.A.R. approach to answering open-ended "Tell me about..." questions

The more difficult questions to answer during an interview are usually the ones that begin with "Tell me about..." because it can be challenging for candidates to get across key points as briefly as possible. During one interview I posed a "Tell me about..." question and the candidate went on and on and then forgot what I'd asked. He stopped, looked confused, and asked, "What was your question again?"

That is why it's important to have some sort of process to follow when answering "Tell me about" questions. The process I taught Taylor has been around as long as I can remember (and no one seems to know who created it). It is called the S.T.A.R. approach, which stands for:

S = Situation: Describe the situation

T = Task: Explain the task or your main goal

A = Action: Tell what actions you took

R = Result: Highlight the positive results and try to quantify them, if at all possible

Here is how the technique works. Let's say the hiring manager asks Taylor, *"Tell me about a situation recently where you exceeded your manager's expectations."* I worked through this example with Taylor to determine how she might respond using the S.T.A.R. method, and here are the results:

Situation: "My manager was getting a lot of pressure from his boss because the order processing rates in our Sales Operations department had been steadily decreasing."

Task: "I was asked to lead a small team focused on finding ways to improve productivity and order accuracy."

Action: "The process improvement team I led focused on three areas: 1) Working with IT to streamline the order entry and validation process, 2)

Creating an "auto-checker" program that would automatically check to make sure all parts of an order were complete before it could be submitted for processing, and 3) Re-training and certifying all department employees on the updated process."

Result: "At the completion of the project, we were able to decrease order-processing time by 52% and increase order accuracy to an all-time record of 98.2%."

Some people find the S.T.A.R. approach to be too difficult to use once they are sitting in front of a hiring manager. If you find it tough during your practice sessions, don't worry – try making your answer shorter by explaining the situation, the actions you took, and the results. Sometimes a simpler, shorter answer is better, and then the hiring manager can always ask a follow up question if there is anything else he or she would like to know.

Use the following **Appendix** template at the back of this book or online as you prepare for your job interview:

- **Interview Preparation Questions (page 273)**

CHAPTER 17
KEY TAKEAWAYS

The best way to ensure you will do well in job interviews is to anticipate interview questions and prepare answers. Most questions will come from five topic groups: Background, job/company/industry, functional fit, style/personality, and future orientation. Recruiters (and some hiring managers) may also ask cultural fit questions. Questions will also come from the "Job Requirements" or "Job Responsibilities" listed in the job posting.

CHAPTER 18

PREPARE QUESTIONS FOR THE EMPLOYER

After anticipating interview questions and preparing your answers, the next step is to prepare your questions for the employer. You definitely don't want to look like a deer in headlights when a hiring manager asks, *"Do you have any questions for me?"* Hiring managers specifically look for candidates who have done their homework and come prepared with questions so they can evaluate whether or not the job and the company will be a good fit for them. Many job seekers forget to do this, making it another great way you can distinguish yourself from other candidates.

Create a list of questions prior to your interview, so you can pull from the list and not worry about your mind going blank at that crucial moment. Choose only a few questions that make the most sense, so you don't overwhelm the hiring manager with too many questions.

As another step to help Taylor (my client mentioned in the last chapter) prepare for her interview, we brainstormed a list of questions to ask the hiring manager during or at the end of her interview to determine if the job, company, and hiring manager's style would fit her own career objectives and work style. Then we grouped the questions into the following categories: hiring manager, job, department, and company. Here is the brainstormed list of Taylor's questions.

Potential questions for the **hiring manager:**
- How would you describe your leadership style?
- What are the reasons you decided to work for this company?
- What keeps you working here?
- What do you like the most and least about working here?

Potential questions about the **job:**

- Is this a newly created position or was there someone previously in it? If someone was in it, what did that person move on to do?
- What do you believe are the most important attributes necessary to be successful in this position? Or, What are the common attributes of the employees who are the most successful in this position?
- What do you believe will be the most challenging aspects of the job? Or, What are the most important tasks/projects I will need to accomplish in my first 90 days on the job?
- How will my job performance be measured? By whom? How often do performance appraisals occur?

Potential questions about the **department:**

- How many people work in this department?
- What is the average tenure for department employees? Or, what is the turnover rate?
- What are the top priorities you're trying to accomplish?
- Would you explain the organizational structure to me (for the department and the company)?

Potential questions about the **company:**

- How would you describe the company culture? The company values?
- What do you see as the company's biggest opportunities?
- How about the biggest threats? (if your research on the company or industry uncovered a threat, explain the threat and then ask how the company will handle it)
- What types of training programs are available to employees at this company?

There are an unlimited number of questions you could ask, but try to keep your list short, with only the questions that matter the most to you, given what you know about the job and the research you've conducted. You might even come up with very specific questions, based on the type of job. For example, if you are interviewing for a sales position, you might ask the hiring manager to explain the sales compensation program and the base pay percentage versus variable pay percentage. Then, you could ask a follow-up question: *"What was the typical variable pay out for all those working in this position last year?"* Remember, ask questions that will help you determine if the job, manager, and company will be a good fit for *you*.

Use the following template at the back of this book or online as you prepare for your job interview:

- **Questions to Ask the Hiring Manager (page 278)**

CHAPTER 18
KEY TAKEAWAYS

Job interviews should be seen as a two-way street. The interviewer's role is to determine if the candidate is the best fit for the position, while the job seeker should use the interview as an opportunity to assess the potential employer. To do this, compose well-thought-out questions to ask during the interview and take time to observe and evaluate not only the hiring manager, but the department and overall company as well.

CONDUCT PRACTICE INTERVIEWS

In addition to preparing potential interview questions and questions you'll ask the hiring manager, asking friends and family members to conduct "mock interviews" is one of the best ways to prepare. It can also be helpful to videotape a few of the practice interviews, so at one of my coaching sessions with Melissa I suggested we do just that. Even though she was nervous about it, Melissa wanted to improve her skills so she agreed.

After we finished, I played the video for Melissa and asked her to tell me about anything she noticed. Here were some of her comments:

"When I shook your hand at the beginning of the interview, I wasn't smiling very much. It kind of looked like I was terrified of you."

"Gosh, I look like a robot in the chair because I was sitting so stiffly."

"Do I really keep crossing and uncrossing my legs like that?"

"Ouch, I looked like I was in pain when I answered that question."

"I really rambled answering that last question. I think I need to practice the S.T.A.R. technique some more."

When you watch yourself on video, it can be a new experience. In Melissa's case, she had done a great job of anticipating and preparing for the hiring manager's questions. *Her problem?* She wasn't polished in interview interaction techniques. Just like Melissa, when you watch yourself on video you'll probably notice things you had absolutely no idea you were doing. If you have access to a video camera or a smart phone with available memory, I suggest you tape yourself going through a few practice interviews, review them, and write down everything you notice.

Practice your interaction

As you conduct your mock interviews, these are important aspects of interaction to practice:

Meeting the interviewer: Mentally tell yourself positive affirmations like you're going to get the job, you believe in yourself, and you look amazing. With these thoughts in mind, a positive mental attitude will show on your face. And don't forget to stand up straight – good posture matters!

Introductory handshake: Always shake his or her hand firmly and with confidence. Look the interviewer in the eyes while shaking hands.

Seating location: Sit in the chair the interviewer points out to you. If the person doesn't point to a chair and you're in a conference room with a large, rectangle table, then attempt to take a chair diagonal to them instead of all the way across the table. Having a large table between you and the hiring manager will make the interview feel more formal and uncomfortable. Sitting at a 90 degree angle to him or her helps reduce some of the space and will make the interview feel more personal and relaxed.

How you sit (body language): Practice finding an easy sitting position that also makes you feel calm, because how you sit can actually demonstrate your level of confidence. Try not to fidget during an interview, as it will draw attention away from the discussion.

Facial expressions: Project a big smile at the beginning of the interview. Then tone it down a bit as you begin the question and answer part. Try to avoid negative facial expressions such as frowning, squinting your eyes, or darting your eyes back and forth. As Melissa noticed by watching her video, her facial expression during one question actually made her look like she was in pain.

Eye contact: Make good eye contact with the interviewer, but don't make it a stare down contest. It is normal to look away every now and again as you think about questions and then look back when you answer.

Personality: Feel free to show your personality. Just make sure the interviewer sees a professional version of the real you.

Gestures: Act natural and be careful of big arm gestures. Avoid crossing your arms across your chest.

Taking notes: It is perfectly fine to bring a notepad of paper and a pen to take notes; I encourage it. Just don't start playing with the pen during the interview.

Rapport with the interviewer: Listen carefully to understand each question, not to immediately reply. Ask clarifying questions if you don't understand something. Don't interrupt and don't get defensive or argue. The goal is to establish a personal connection with the hiring manager or recruiter.

"Fluff" phrases: Eliminate these types of phrases from your vocabulary... "Quite frankly," "To be honest with you," "Just between you and me," etc. These are what I call "fluff" phrases because they aren't needed and, worse yet, can tend to make you seem dishonest or arrogant.

Pause technique: Don't ramble when answering questions. Instead, learn to use pauses effectively to help the flow of the discussion.

S.T.A.R. technique: Use the S.T.A.R. method (discussed in Chapter 17) for answering "Tell me about..." questions. Practice the process until it becomes effortless.

One area I asked Melissa to work on was pacing the interviewer. Each hiring manager has a different style and speed with which they conduct interviews. The goal of the job seeker is to match the interviewer's pace. For example, you might have a hiring manager (like me) who is very fast paced. They speak fast, their movements are fast, and just about everything about them is fast (I even drink coffee fast). If you answer questions very slowly and go into minute detail with your answers, you'll most likely bore him or her. Flex your style to better match the interviewer.

On the other side, you might end up with a hiring manager whose pace is slow. They walk slowly, move slowly, ask questions slowly and deliberately – everything they do is at a slow pace and they love details, details, and more details. If your normal style is fast, then as the job candidate you'll need to slow yourself down a bit when interacting with this hiring manager. You'll also need to provide more detailed answers than you might otherwise give.

Avoid nonverbal mistakes

As Melissa and I conducted additional practice interviews, she began feeling more comfortable with interviewing. This allowed her to relax and enjoy the process, even making me laugh as she shared funny work stories. Once she felt comfortable with everything she was trying to remember to do during interviews, we switched directions and discussed seven nonverbal mistakes that job seekers should avoid to improve their chances of interview success. These include:

Unusual handshake. A "limp fish" handshake (too soft) can portray insecurity, while a "handshake of steel" (too hard) can project arrogance. A handshake lasting way too long tells hiring managers the candidate might be trying overly hard to impress him or her and that the person might stretch the truth about their accomplishments, knowledge, or experience. Practice your handshaking *before* you get to the interview so you won't even have to worry about it.

Poor or too much eye contact. Poor eye contact can signify that you aren't interested in the position. At the other end of the spectrum, too much eye contact can be intimidating and turn the interview into a stare down. One of the most awkward interviews I've ever conducted was with a job candidate who never looked away from my face or seemingly blinked. Keep eye contact casual and relaxed, not creepy.

Out of control gestures. These include constantly tapping a foot, shaking a leg, clicking a pen, twirling a strand of hair, or too many hand and arm gestures. They take attention away from you and what you're saying. I once interviewed a woman who kept using gigantic arm gestures while she talked. She knocked over both our cups of coffee on the conference room table… and the interview went downhill from there.

Lack of facial expression. Humans have emotions, so when you don't smile or emote any type of positive facial expression during an interview, it can be a turnoff for hiring managers. Try imagining the interview as a typical conversation with a friend – and don't be afraid to show your personality. Really. It is okay to laugh and even make a funny comment every now and then. Like I've mentioned before, hiring managers want to hire real people, not robots.

Poor posture (body language). Leaning back and crossing your arms and/or legs can make you come across as either uninterested or arrogant. I conducted an interview once where the job candidate kept leaning way back in his chair and rocking the chair onto the back two legs. At one point, he leaned so far back that he almost fell over. So sit up, lean forward slightly, and at least try to look like you're fully engaged in the conversation.

Odd attire. Clothing can have a negative impact if it is too inconsistent with the position or the company culture. I once interviewed a man for a marketing manager job at a conservative medical equipment company who came to the interview dressed like John Travolta in the movie "Saturday Night Fever." His unbuttoned shirt, exposed hairy chest, and loads of necklaces just didn't fit the job, company, or industry.

Too much perfume. It should go without saying – don't wear any perfume or scented lotions to job interviews, but I'm going to say it anyway because it happens a lot. One female candidate had on so much perfume that I had to excuse myself from my office for several minutes to wipe my tearing eyes. Another job seeker (male) wore so much cologne that I could still smell it in the conference room several hours after he had left. Hiring managers should remember you, not your perfume.

While I've never made hiring decisions based solely on a candidate's nonverbal communication, I use the cues to help me see the big picture and to uncover inconsistencies or potential issues. To increase your chances of interview success, be consciously aware of your nonverbal communication and avoid these mistakes.

A final takeaway for practicing your interview skills

Hiring managers want to hire real people. I've said this previously, but it's so important and so many people miss the opportunity to showcase their unique personalities during a job interview. So again, don't be afraid to be yourself during interviews and to inject your personality or sense of humor into the discussion. You'll most likely spend more time with your coworkers and boss than you will your family or friends, so share your true self with the hiring manager, and take time to make sure the job, employer, and boss are also a good fit for you.

As you conduct your mock interviews, try using the **Practice Interview Scoring Sheet (page 280)** in the **Appendix** of this book. This document allows the "hiring manager" from the practice interview to check off whether the "candidate" is remembering to achieve certain things and behave certain ways. After each practice interview, ask the person role-playing with you to fill out the sheet and discuss their comments so you can continue to improve your interview skills.

CHAPTER 19
KEY TAKEAWAYS

To prepare for job interviews, conduct "mock" interview sessions with family members and friends. Ask them to role-play the hiring manager with you as the job candidate, and then have them assess your interview skills. Pace your interviewer. Be sure to pay careful attention to the content of your answers as well as your nonverbal communication.

PREPARE TO ANSWER THE TOUGHEST INTERVIEW QUESTIONS

Now that you've conducted several mock interviews with family members and friends, let's focus on how to handle three of the interview questions that make most job seekers cringe and want to run for the hills to hide:

"What's your biggest weakness?"

"How much money do you currently make?"

"What's your game plan to ensure your success in the job?"

The biggest weakness question

Hiring managers love to ask the *"What's your biggest weakness?"* question because a candidate's answers usually tells him or her three things: 1) Their level of self-awareness, 2) How they handle obstacles and respond to issues, and 3) How much they know about the position for which they are interviewing.

I had a new client, Laura, who told me this story about a previous job interview: During the interview, she was asked to explain her biggest weakness. Laura wasn't prepared to answer the question and her mind went blank. So she quickly made up a weakness. *Her problem?* The weakness Laura chose off the top of her head happened to be the most important skill required for the position. Oops! Shortly after she responded, the hiring manager ended the interview.

Don't let the same situation happen during your next job interview. Review your personal S.W.O.T. analysis results (Chapter 7) and consider your current and past weaknesses. Then, think through how you could handle the question in one of the following three ways:

Option #1: Explain a weakness you've already worked on improving. Example: *"I used to be incredibly nervous when it came to public speaking. Last year I joined Toastmaster's and realized how much fun it could be once I better understood the process and how to prepare for presentations. Now I actually look forward to speaking in front of groups."*

This answer lets the hiring manager know you've considered your weaknesses, determined ways to overcome them, and then described the actions you took to improve yourself.

Option #2: Explain an attitude difference. Example: *"Because I absolutely hate missing deadlines and try to complete all projects ahead of schedule, sometimes I get impatient with other people when they don't seem to have the same sense of urgency that I do. I recently read an interesting book about social styles at work and I've been practicing ways to flex my style with other people's styles."*

This answer demonstrates your understanding of how a positive trait could cause friction with others. It also explains how you're learning from it and the actions you've taken to be able to work better with others.

Option #3: Briefly explain your personal development plan. Example: *"As part of my ongoing personal development, every year I analyze my strengths and weaknesses and then choose one area on which to focus. This year I've been working on improving my strategic planning skills. Last year I worked on learning how to manage budgets and read financials, and the year before I focused on improving my presentation skills."*

This answer shows your ability to analyze your assets and liabilities. It also demonstrates your dedication to continuous improvement and learning – qualities most managers look for in high-performing employees.

The salary question

Now we'll look at a question that tends to be asked later in the job interview – the salary question. Imagine you're sitting in a job interview and everything has been great. You're feeling really good about your answers so far, and then the hiring manager asks, *"How much money do you currently make?"*

or *"How much salary do you expect to make in this position?"* Your heart races and you begin to sweat. How should you answer?

As a recent mentee of mine discovered, salary can be a difficult topic to discuss if you haven't first conducted some research and thought through a response. James felt like he'd been close to getting the job during two interviews. But the inevitable *"What do you make in your current position?"* question came up and James told the truth. In both cases, the hiring managers shared that his current salary was more than the position could pay.

"What is the best way to respond to this question?" James asked me. *"After I told them my current pay, I let both hiring managers know I'm flexible with salary. But it seemed like once they heard what I'm currently making, they kind of switched off and didn't consider me a viable candidate anymore."*

As a job seeker, think of this question like a poker game. In poker, the goal is to get the other players to lay their cards on the table before you show your own cards. The same is true during an interview. Your goal is to get the hiring manager or recruiter to lay down their cards on the table first by sharing the salary range. Because, as James found out, once you share a specific salary number, you might price yourself too high (or too low) for the position.

Here are tips to help you prepare for the salary question and discussion during job interviews:

Tip #1: Arm yourself with salary information. Before you go to the job interview, spend adequate time researching average salaries and salary ranges for similar jobs in your area, industry, and geography. There are many websites that provide this information, including: salary.com, payscale.com, glassdoor.com, jobsearchintelligence.com, indeed.com, and careeronestop.org.

Tip #2: Deflect the salary question if it is asked early in the job interview. It won't do you any good to tell the hiring manager your current pay or a desired salary range if you haven't at least gone through the interview to see if you and the hiring manager believe you're a good fit. Consider letting him or her know that you'd like to better understand the job responsibilities and requirements and how well you meet those needs before discussing the salary topic.

Tip #3: Be prepared to provide a salary range. This can be handled in a few different ways. You could provide the salary range you've researched, as in, *"Based on my research, similar positions in this geography and industry are currently paying between $x and $y. Is this also the range you've budgeted for this position?"* Or, you could share the salary range you desire, such as, *"Based on the job requirements we discussed and my knowledge, skills, and experience, I would expect the salary range to be between $x and $y."*

Tip #4: Think about how much you'd like to make. This means trying to avoid sharing an exact number, because it can place you above or below the budgeted salary for the position. Instead, provide a range you'd like to make. *"Because I'm changing industries, I'm not expecting to exactly match my previous salary, but I'd like my pay to be in the range of…"*

Tip #5: Think about ways you could side step the question. Remember, the goal is to get the hiring manager or recruiter to tell you the budgeted range for the job before you share any salary information. Try to avoid giving out information by providing answers such as, *"My research shows similar positions pay in the range of $x to $y. I'm sure you've budgeted a salary range based on competitive data for this industry. What is your budgeted range?"* Or, *"If I'm the candidate you'd prefer for this position, I'm sure we'll be able to reach agreement on the salary, as I'm willing to be flexible. What is the budgeted salary range?"*

Tip #6: Discuss the salary range with the HR rep during the initial screening interview. You don't have to wait until you've made it to the interview round with the hiring manager. The initial telephone screen with the HR recruiter is a great time to discuss the job's pay range to make sure your expectations are within the salary parameters. This also makes the salary discussion with the hiring manager much less stressful when it comes up.

Tip #7: Define the lowest salary amount you'd be willing to accept. An important aspect of any negotiation is defining the point at which you'll walk away. Take time to think about the lowest salary you'd be willing to accept and why. Remember this amount when it comes time to negotiate your starting salary.

Tip #8: Don't lie about your compensation. It is never a good idea to lie about your salary. The business world is actually a lot smaller than you'd think, and you might be surprised at how easy it is for a manager to find out salary and benefit information. That is why I recommend you conduct salary research and provide your salary range expectations for the position, instead of your current salary.

Many clients have told me they wished it were illegal for companies to request their current salary information. I understand how they feel. The reason recruiters and hiring managers ask job candidates for this information is because they know former employers won't divulge compensation information. Most companies will only reveal previous employment dates and confirm job titles for past employment.

Why you get asked the salary question

Most recruiters and hiring managers don't ask the salary question because they want to make you the lowest possible job offer. You get asked about your current salary information because hiring managers want to pay a salary that is fair, both to the external marketplace and to the internal employees already working at the company.

If you are the candidate he or she wants to hire, they will aim to be competitive with their offer. That is because hiring a candidate at a salary much lower (or higher) than others working in the same position at the company can create issues later, if employees share information. It is in the best interest of the employer to maintain harmony for compensation within similar positions – with higher salaries paid only for very specific reasons, such as special skill sets or geographic uplifts, which is slightly higher pay for employees located in high expense cities, such as New York.

Having some inside information into the way a hiring manager determines salary will hopefully ease your apprehension of this question. As a hiring manager, before I ever made a job offer to my top candidate, I would ask about his or her current salary or find out the target salary range the person was willing to accept. Once I had this information, it was much easier to look at the group of employees currently working in the same or similar positions and make comparisons.

I would sit down with my recruiter or HR business partner and consider the salaries for the current employees, their education, work experience, and performance levels as well as outside competitive salary data within our industry. Then we would compare this to the job candidate I wanted to hire to determine the most competitive compensation I could offer, while still maintaining harmony within the current team. It was a well-thought-out process that tried to take the most important factors into consideration, and I always took the time to explain to the candidate how I came up with their salary offer when I made them the job offer.

If you're the candidate a hiring manager wants to hire, you'll likely be asked the salary question. It is your choice as to how you want to handle it, based on how comfortable you're feeling with the hiring manager. As my mentee James found out, sometimes honesty isn't always the best policy and you'll want to share a desired salary range instead. No matter how you proceed, be sure you've conducted adequate research, think about how you might respond, and always be professional and polite in your approach. This will help you walk away much closer to your preferred salary.

The game plan question

One of my favorite interview questions as a hiring manager is, *"What's your game plan to ensure your success in the job?"* because it quickly reveals the proactive candidates – the ones who have thought through what it will take to be successful in the role. Not having a well-thought-out answer to this question is a quick way to get eliminated from the hiring process. If you've followed the process I've taught throughout this book, you won't have that problem. Why? Because you've already done all the prep work that will help you determine what it will take to be successful and create your plan of action.

Remember my client Amanda, from Chapter 4? She had narrowed down her target jobs to two: 1) Pharmaceutical sales rep, and 2) Dental equipment sales rep. Before her pharmaceutical sales interview, I had Amanda brainstorm what it would take for her to be successful, based on the job description and requirements, her job shadowing, and her research. Here are a few of Amanda's answers:

Amanda: *"I know I'll need to learn everything about the products I'll be representing so the customers will see me as knowledgeable and I'll be able to earn their trust."*

Amanda: *"To be successful, I'll also need to quickly learn about my sales territory and all my customers. I think it would help me if I could go on a ride-along with an experienced sales rep at the company, so I can see their sales techniques in action and learn from them."*

Amanda: *"I'll also need training on the computer systems I'll be using in the job, to make sure I'm doing everything I'm supposed to do as part of the position."*

Based on our discussion, I had Amanda create a brief, written game plan that listed the key actions she would need to take to ensure her success in the job. After a few additions and tweaks, she had a nicely formatted one page document she could show and discuss with the hiring manager during her job interview. Here is her game plan:

Amanda's New Hire Game Plan to Ensure Success

- *Products:* Learn everything there is to know about the products I'll be representing.
- *Terminology:* Learn all the appropriate medical terminology that customers will use with me during our discussions. Obtain recommendations from my manager on the best ways to gain this knowledge, be it on the job, through reading articles, attending seminars, memorizing terminology and definitions, etc.
- *Sales territory:* Learn my sales territory as well as background information about all of my customers within my territory.
- *Sales techniques:* Learn sales techniques from one of the top company representatives – my preference is to ride along with one or two reps for several days to observe them and be able to ask questions.
- *Company computer systems and processes:* Learn all the computer systems and software programs that are used as part of this job. Ensure understanding of all processes and outcomes.
- *Marketing tools:* Learn about all the marketing tools that are available for use during the sales process, the best times to use them, and for which customers or situations.
- *Resource people:* Meet all the various groups and people who will be helpful resources, such as immediate team members, internal support staff, marketing team, etc.
- *Communication with manager:* Find out my manager's preferred communication methods and what I can do to ensure we work well together.

- *Performance criteria:* Speak with my manager to clearly understand the criteria on which my performance will be judged as well as how and when my manager will determine if I'm successful in my job.

When you go through the process of determining your own game plan for the position in which you'll be interviewing, ask yourself: *"What will it take for me to be successful?"* Re-read the job description with the list of job requirements and skills/experience necessary. Then, using that information and your research, brainstorm a list of items (like Amanda did) and put these items into a one-page document with a brief explanation of each item. Once you've completed your game plan, print out a few copies and bring it with you to your job interview. You'll impress the hiring manager when you pull it out and review it with him or her.

A side note – never speak negatively about past jobs or bosses

Before I conclude this chapter, I want to bring up the importance of never speaking negatively about past jobs or previous managers – no matter how much you might have disliked either. I know some hiring managers who will purposely ask interview candidates to tell them about the worst aspects of working for a previous company or boss. Heads up! These are trick questions to see if you'll speak negatively about a past job, employer, or manager. Answering these types of questions can be difficult, especially if you're leaving an unhappy work environment or really do work for a terrible boss. While you might like to let loose and vent, a job interview isn't the time or place – save your angry tirade for a confidential discussion with your best friend.

My advice in answering negative questions is to try your best to turn your answer around into positive comments. Let's say a hiring manager asks you to explain the top three things you hated the most in a previous job. In your head you might be thinking: *My boss was a jerk who wasn't supportive of my career development, my work assignments were boring and pure drudgery, and I was severely underpaid with no opportunity for pay raises or bonus compensation* – don't say this out loud!

Instead, say something like: *"I'm looking for a job where I have a boss who is supportive of my career development, who will give me projects and assignments*

that are challenging and will help me improve my skills, and where I have oppor-
tunities to earn pay raises or bonus compensation based on my work performance."

If a hiring manager puts further pressure on you to explain negative aspects of a job, boss, or employer, and you feel uncomfortable with the request – tell him or her that. Say something like, *"I'd rather not focus on the negative attributes. No job or manager is perfect, and I prefer to see situations as learning opportunities..."*

When you desperately want the job for which you're interviewing, it can be tempting to provide the hiring manager with the answers they want to hear. To avoid being caught off guard by trick questions, always maintain the highest level of integrity and avoid speaking negatively about past jobs, bosses, or employers.

Negative comments from candidates during job interviews are unappealing to hiring managers because it causes them to wonder if you'll speak badly about them or the company one day. So stay away from comments that bad mouth past jobs or bosses and, if possible, focus your answers on the positive aspects you look forward to in the new job.

CHAPTER 20
KEY TAKEAWAYS

Come prepared to interviews ready to handle the toughest questions by thinking through your strategy first. For the, "What's your biggest weakness?" question, consider your current and past weaknesses and what you've done to overcome them. For the, "What salary are you expecting for this position?" question, avoid sharing what you currently make so you won't price yourself too high or too low for the job. Share a desired salary range instead. Prepare your game plan for success in the job before you arrive at the job interview. And no matter what, never speak negatively about a previous employer or boss.

PRACTICE WATCHING THE HIRING MANAGER'S NONVERBAL CUES FOR IMPORTANT CLUES

I had coffee one weekend with a friend who had recently gone to a job interview. When I asked Erin what the interviewer thought of her, she didn't know. *Her problem?* Erin had been so nervous during the interview that she'd forgotten to pay attention to the hiring manager's nonverbal communication.

That happens a lot. Many people are so worried about how they come across during an interview that they forget to watch the body language of their interviewer. But being able to read nonverbal cues can increase your chances of interview success.

Why? The way a hiring manager reacts to your comments and moves his or her body can demonstrate whether they are listening or bored, whether or not they agree with what you're saying, and if they believe you would be a good fit for the job. So the next time you are in an in-person job interview or video interview, try looking for these nonverbal cues:

Facial expression: If the interviewer is smiling and looks interested in what you're saying – great! If he or she appears confused (furrowed eyebrow or one eyebrow raised), disgusted (both eyebrows raised and shakes head side to side) or uninterested (unexpressive face or glazed eyes) – take note and adjust your behavior, such as quickly wrapping up your answer if his or her facial expression shows boredom.

Eye contact: If the interview is going well, the hiring manager should be making regular eye contact. Pay attention to cues that could indicate things are going awry, such as the interviewer looking around the room, glancing at the clock on the wall, or looking down at their watch or notepad a lot. These behaviors could mean you're rambling, that he/she is ready to move on to the next question, or that they've already made a decision about you as a candidate.

Posture: Ideally, the hiring manager's posture should be relaxed and leaning forward, demonstrating engagement and interest. If the interviewer's posture is stiff, or if they lean back and cross their arms, beware. These cues can signify anxiety or discomfort and could indicate they don't believe you're a good fit for the job or that your answers aren't believable.

Gestures: Positive gestures to look for are taking notes, nodding "yes," and laughing at your funny stories. Cues to watch out for are a cocked head to one side with a raised eyebrow, and shaking their head "no" while verbally responding "yes."

If you're unsure of something you've just noticed during your interview, don't be afraid to check in with the hiring manager. You could say something such as: *"It looks like I might have confused you with my answer. Were you looking for specific examples or for my overall philosophy about people management?"* Or, *"Did that answer your question or was there something else you were looking for?"* Then listen to their answer before deciding how you should proceed.

CHAPTER 21
KEY TAKEAWAYS

To increase your chances of job interview success, practice reading the nonverbal cues of hiring managers. Look at facial expressions, eye contact, posture, and gestures for important clues as to how you're doing during the interview – then modify your behavior accordingly.

LEARN TO CLOSE THE INTERVIEW WITH CLASS

After I videotaped Rebecca during a practice interview, we sat down and watched how she did. When it was over I turned and asked her, *"Did you get the job?"*

Rebecca seemed perplexed. *"What do you mean?"*

"You thanked the hiring manager at the end of the interview, shook hands, and then left. But did you get the job?" I asked. *"What I mean is do you know how the hiring manager felt about your qualifications for the job?"*

Rebecca stared at me for a long moment. *"Well, I think I did okay because the nonverbal communication of the hiring manager seemed positive,"* she replied. *"You were leaning forward and nodded your head yes several times when I was answering questions."*

"Excellent! That's a great start," I said with an encouraging smile. *"But at the end of the interview when the hiring manager asked if you had any questions, how did you respond?"*

With pride in her voice, Rebecca responded, *"I asked three of my pre-written questions to find out more about the culture of the company, what a typical day was like in the job, and what I would be evaluated on to determine if I was successful."*

"Good. But did you get the job or find out the next steps in the hiring process so you'd know what to expect when you walked out of the interview?" I asked. This is one of my favorite tips to share with clients. I know it is a critical step to the interview process, but most interviewees never do it!

Rebecca understood my point. *"Oops! I don't know if I got the job or not. Can I really find that out at the end of an interview?"*

In every interview the job seeker's goal is to sell herself to the hiring manager and to evaluate if the position is a good two-way fit. But don't forget... if you decide during the interview that you want the job, try to discover where you stand with the hiring manager and find out the next steps in the hiring process.

There always seems to be a big debate on whether or not a candidate should try to "close the sale" at the end of a job interview. As a hiring manager, it always shocked me that so few people did this. Closing an interview appropriately is the only way to determine where you stand in obtaining the job, what the hiring manager thinks of your qualifications, or where your interviewer is in the hiring process.

Don't sound like a dishonest used car salesperson

The one caveat is you must close an interview the right way or you'll end up sounding like a dishonest used car salesperson. These are a few of the worst interview wrap-up comments I've heard:

"If you're looking for the best candidate, then that's me! I recommend you hire me right now."

"I believe my background and experience are a perfect fit and I'm willing to consider your best offer!"

"Why don't we just wrap up this interview right now and have me start work on Monday?"

"Since I'm obviously the best candidate for the job, how much are you going to pay me for a sign-on bonus?"

See what I mean? These comments come off as a shady sales pitch, which is definitely not what you want to portray in an interview. Professionalism and tact are of the utmost importance when it comes to closing a job interview, and my preference is to take an open, honest approach.

Find out what the hiring manager thinks

After the hiring manager has asked if you have any questions and you've discussed those, consider asking one of the following three questions:

1. "Based on my background and the skills and experience we discussed, how well do I fit the profile of the candidate you're looking for?"

This question will help you find out what the hiring manager thinks of your background and whether or not they believe you're a good fit.

2. "Given what you know about me, how do I compare to the other candidates you've interviewed?"

This question will help you understand how you compare to the other candidates in terms of education, experience, skills, or knowledge. It should also help you determine what the hiring manager thinks about you.

3. Given what we've just discussed during this interview, do you have any concerns about my fit for this position?"

This is my favorite of the three questions. It is a reverse question because it tries to uncover any issues that might hold the interviewer back from hiring you (that they might not otherwise have shared with you).

Once you have the answer to your question, you'll be in a much better position to determine your next move. For example, if the hiring manager brought up any concerns about your fit for the position, this is a good time to discuss those. It gives you the opportunity to (quickly) alleviate any issues with further explanation about your experience, education, or skills.

Ask about the next steps

If the hiring manager provides positive feedback, consider asking one of these follow up questions:

"What are the next steps in the hiring process?"

This will help you verify where the hiring manager is in the hiring process; such as do they have more candidates to interview or are you the last one? How soon will they be making a decision?

"Would you like my list of references and letters of recommendation?"

This will also help draw out where you stand with the hiring manager. A good answer is *"Yes."* A bad response is when the hiring manager says, *"No thank you"* or *"Not at this time."*

Reiterate your interest in the position

Finally, at the very end, close the interview by reiterating your interest in the position. Here are two suggested methods:

"Based on my research and what we've discussed, I would really like to work for you in this job. How soon until you'll be making a decision?"

This closing lets the interviewer know you believe you're a good fit for the position and confirms that you want to work there. It also helps you uncover any additional decision-makers.

"This discussion has made me even more excited about this job opportunity and I would love to be the person you hire. Is there anything else you need from me before you make a decision?"

This closing also demonstrates that you want to work for the company and can uncover anything else needed to move the process along, such as providing your reference list or letters of recommendation.

Thank the hiring manager

After using the most appropriate closing questions and comments, don't forget to thank the hiring manager for his or her time and ask for a business card before you leave the interview. By obtaining a business card, you will have their correctly spelled name, title, mailing address, telephone number, and email address to use when you write your thank you note. If you forget to obtain their business card, check with your HR contact to ensure you have the hiring manager's correct information.

After teaching Rebecca the different ways to professionally close a job interview, we spent time practicing. *"Now I understand what you meant when you asked me if I'd gotten the job. And I can't believe the difference it makes,"* she gushed. *"This way I leave the interview with a good idea of where I stand with the hiring manager and what to expect for the next steps, instead of leaving and wondering how I did."* Exactly!

CHAPTER 22 KEY TAKEAWAYS

Don't leave a job interview wondering where you stand with the hiring manager. Practice the techniques to professionally close an interview so the hiring manager realizes you want the job and so you leave the interview knowing the next steps in the hiring process.

ENSURE ALL DOCUMENTS ARE READY FOR THE INTERVIEW

Jenna arrived at her job interview confident and excited. As she sat down in the chair across from the hiring manager he glanced down at his desk and then looked back up at Jenna. *"Oh, I don't have a copy of your resume with me. Do you have an extra one with you?"* he asked. *Jenna's problem?* She forgot to bring copies of her resume.

You'd be surprised how many times throughout my career I've gone on job interviews where hiring managers didn't even have a copy of my resume or the application I had already submitted. This recently happened to a client and, thankfully, she had several extra copies she'd printed out and brought with her.

Being prepared with key documents can improve your chances for a successful interview. For example, by bringing an extra resume for yourself, you can glance down at it to quickly identify jobs or projects to use as examples when answering questions. By bringing a portfolio of work examples you can show proof of your expertise and skills. Using a notepad and pen to take notes during the interview will help you ensure you don't forget to discuss something important the hiring manager mentioned. Like most things in life, it is always better to be over-prepared than under-prepared.

Here is a list of the most important items you should bring to job interviews:

Your resume. Bring three to four copies of your resume, because you never know when you'll be asked to interview with others from the department or with the hiring manager's boss. It is always best to have more copies than you'll need.

Your reference list. Same as your resume – bring extra copies.

Recommendation letters. You won't need as many copies of these, but they make a great "leave behind" for the hiring manager to review after your interview. Let's say you have three recommendation letters; make at least two sets (and staple each set together) and leave the originals at home.

The job description. Print the original job description and bring a copy with you to the interview.

Portfolio of work. Examples of your work can be a helpful way to demonstrate your expertise – see Chapter 12. Use this to help set yourself apart from other job seekers and to demonstrate the quality of your work to hiring managers.

Paper and pen. Always, always, always bring a notepad and pen. Before you take any notes, ask the interviewer if it is okay for you to do so during the interview.

Thank you note cards. Before going on interviews, make sure you've already purchased appropriate thank you cards. "Appropriate" means the cards look professional and will work well for the industry and company where you'll be interviewing. For example, don't use wedding thank you notes (usually silver lettering on white paper with flowing, script-like font styles). Don't bring them to the interview, but have them ready to use as soon as you get home. Note: Depending on how high-tech the industry or the employer is, an email thank you note might be more appropriate.

Other items to consider, in case you're offered (and you accept) the position on the spot:

Driver's license. Your driver's license is a picture identification document. You'll need this when you're asked to fill out the HR paperwork.

Passport. Many companies now ask for two picture identification documents for verification purposes.

Social Security card. Some employers might allow you to simply write down your Social Security number, but most require signed verification that an HR employee has seen the card (many will make a copy of it).

Fact sheet. Create this for yourself before your interview. It should list the names, addresses, phone numbers and work dates for each job you've held. Many companies ask for this information as part of their new-hire paperwork because it aids them in conducting background checks before officially hiring a candidate.

Showing up for interviews with the appropriate documents (and extra copies) will help you feel more prepared and confident, and, you'll be ready to fill out the HR paperwork when you've been offered the job.

A final tip for interview success – envision success

After you've prepared all the documents you'll want to bring to your interview, don't forget about getting a good night's sleep. You'll want to show up refreshed, relaxed, and energetic – plan your time wisely so you can get to sleep early the night before your interview. As you're drifting off to sleep, picture yourself at your interview. Think positive thoughts. In your mind, see yourself sitting in the interview and answering questions. You are laughing with the interviewer, having a great discussion, and feeling excited and happy when you leave. Envision receiving a call from the hiring manager with a job offer. By visualizing your success, you will be even more apt to make it come true.

**CHAPTER 23
KEY TAKEAWAYS**

Showing up with the appropriate documents is a key part of being prepared for interviews and obtaining job offers. This includes having multiple copies of your resume, reference list, and recommendation letters, your driver's license, social security card or number, passport, portfolio of work, notepad and pen, and fact sheet. Don't leave home without them.

DRESS FOR POSITIVE IMPACT

Cynthia was excited about her two upcoming job interviews, but she was struggling with what to wear. Both interviews were with large, global corporations, but their work environments were at opposite ends of the spectrum. One was a conservative and formal office environment where most people wore suits and typical business attire. The other was much more casual, and most employees wore jeans and t-shirts to work.

"I'll definitely wear a business suit to the first interview, but I'm really confused about what to wear for the second one," she told me one afternoon. *"I mean, I can't show up for a job interview wearing jeans and a cotton t-shirt, can I?"*

Cynthia's problem? She didn't know anyone who worked at the second company, so the only information she had were pictures she saw posted on the company's website. What you wear to an interview can create an image or perception of the type of person you are, and as Cynthia realized, choosing her attire was an important part of presenting herself as the right candidate to hire.

How to choose interview attire

Over the years, workplace clothing has shifted. The dot-com era ushered in a more casual approach, which included interview attire. When the economic recession hit, however, job seekers began dressing up as a way to differentiate themselves from other candidates. The recession also created a heightened awareness in hiring managers of what candidates wear to interviews. Their attire is now often seen as a test of the candidate's familiarity with the company and industry. Believe it or not, your clothes *can and do* influence your chances of landing a job.

For example, if you wore a black pantsuit to an interview in Florida in the middle of August, the hiring manager might think you've lost your mind. Why? The attire isn't appropriate for the geographic location or time of year.

What if a woman wore a navy pantsuit, pulled her hair into a low ponytail, wore little makeup, no jewelry, and flat shoes to a job interview as a clothing stylist? It is doubtful she'd be offered the job because the hiring manager will be looking for someone who projects an image of creativity with clothing, makeup, and accessories that are fashion-forward.

Wearing a nice outfit isn't enough if you really want to score a job offer. Your attire must show the hiring manager that you understand the industry, company, and job for which you're interviewing. If you were interviewing with a large bank, you'd likely want to wear a conservative, dark colored business suit. If you showed up wearing an array of brightly colored, trendy clothes, this would definitely decrease your chances of getting hired.

On the flip side, showing up to an interview wearing a dark, conservative business suit for a job that requires creativity and "quirkiness," like creative director at a cutting-edge, forward thinking design firm, would yield the same results.

Here is an example of image perception in action and how it can hurt your career, especially when interviewing for a job. One day while I was working for a Fortune 500 medical equipment manufacturer, I went into the break room to buy a snack. As I walked up to the vending machine I overheard the conversation of a group of women in their mid-twenties. One woman commented, *"I just can't believe no one around here seems to take me seriously. I'm obviously the best person for the job. I'm the fastest, most skilled, and most knowledgeable out of everyone who applied. I just can't believe they didn't give the job to me!"*

As I turned around to leave the break room, I glanced over at the woman who had made the comments. She was wearing a pair of low waist jeans, her hair was cropped short and spiked, there was a ring through her left eyebrow, and a large tattoo became visible on her lower back when she reached across the table for a napkin. This might seem like an extreme example, but if you were a hiring manager at this large, conservative company, how would you perceive this woman based on her appearance? If the position required interaction with external customers that included physicians and hospital administrators, would you feel comfortable having her as a "face" of your company?

The worst part about this example is the woman interviewing for the open position already worked at the company, so she should have been familiar with the culture, environment, and the appropriate attire to wear to a job interview. One of the biggest mistakes I see as a career coach (and former hiring manager) are job seekers who don't conduct adequate research on what they should wear to their job interview. If it doesn't fit with the company culture or industry, showing up in a suit *could* be as detrimental to your chances of obtaining a job as wearing an outfit like the example above!

Here are tips I discussed with Cynthia, to help her create a positive impact through her interview attire:

- As the examples show, the appropriate attire depends on the job, the company, and the industry in which you'll be interviewing.
- Your attire should also be geographically and seasonally appropriate – you wouldn't wear the same outfit to a summertime interview in Arizona as you would in winter in New York.
- Research the company, industry, and competitors to determine suitable interview outfits.
- Consider the job type (engineer, sales rep, marketing) and level (individual contributor, manager, director, vice president) to help you decide on the most appropriate interview attire.
- Still unsure of what to wear? Call the company's HR department and ask what they recommend.
- When in doubt, err on the side of being slightly overdressed, rather than show up looking too casual.
- Don't have an appropriate outfit? Go to a large department store like Nordstrom or Macy's and ask for help from a personal shopper, which are typically free, or hire a local stylist.
- Ensure your clothes are cleaned and pressed.
- Avoid wearing perfume or scented lotions.
- Wear makeup and jewelry that are appropriate for the job.

- If you are worried about the outfit you've chosen, put it on and ask the opinion of a few friends you trust who will give you their honest opinion.

After our coaching session, Cynthia called the HR department at the second company. The HR representative was very helpful, even asking her which department and with which manager she would be interviewing. Then she provided several examples of what would be appropriate interview attire.

After thanking her for the help, Cynthia hired a local personal wardrobe stylist. Armed with the information from the HR representative, she met the stylist at a nearby shopping mall and they spent three hours together. Cynthia tried on clothes and explored different looks from multiple stores.

At the end of the style session Cynthia was both relieved and ecstatic – she found her interview outfit for the second company. She chose a high-end pair of dark colored jeans that looked like trousers, a brightly colored silk blouse, a cropped jacket to wear over the blouse, and a chic pair of heels with a statement necklace. *"Who says casual has to be boring?"* Cynthia said, while she modeled her new outfit for me at our next session. *"This outfit will definitely give the hiring manager a good first impression."*

The importance of making a good first impression

Did you know it takes only three to five seconds for someone to form a first impression? And while you might wish that opinion were based on your intelligence or experience, most studies show that first impressions are shaped by what can be seen or heard in those initial few seconds. What impression might you give when meeting a hiring manager?

I first met my client Tiffany over the telephone. She was intelligent, funny, and highly qualified for the positions she had applied for online. But for some reason, Tiffany wasn't receiving the job offers she expected after leaving the interviews. We took the time to analyze everything she had done to prepare for each interview, reviewed her resume in detail, and discussed the interview questions and her answers. Nothing stood out to me as a potential reason why she wasn't receiving job offers.

Then we met in person. *Her problem?* Tiffany was what I would call a "free spirit" who loved wearing bright, casual clothing, lots of makeup, and layers of jewelry – but she was interviewing for jobs in large, formal companies where the majority of employees wore suits. At first, Tiffany didn't like the idea of toning down her image for interviews because she was afraid she might lose her unique "look." It was clear Tiffany needed some guidance on the do's and don'ts of interview attire.

We went through her wardrobe together and, keeping in mind that it was April in Seattle, which means a lot of rain, we decided on a pair of tan silk slacks, a leopard print silk blouse under a stylish black blazer, and a pair of sleek, black patent leather high heels. Tiffany also went a little lighter on her makeup and switched her fingernail polish from orange to a French manicure. Then we topped off her outfit with a tan trench coat and matching umbrella (it really *does* rain a lot here in Seattle) and a sleek briefcase.

The result? Tiffany was able to maintain her unique personal style while fitting into the fairly formal and conservative company environments where she was interviewing. After those few adjustments to tone down her overall look, making it more appropriate for the industry and company where she wanted to work, Tiffany began receiving those much-coveted job offers.

To ensure a positive first impression at a job interview, it is imperative to proactively manage your image. Here are five tips to help you do just that:

Tip #1: Analyze your attire. Do your clothes create an appropriate personal image? If you are trying to cultivate an executive presence for a job in management, are you dressing to look the part? If you want the hiring manager to view you as creative, do your clothing and jewelry choices reflect your individual creativity? Personal shoppers and stylists are great resources to help you upgrade your wardrobe or change your overall "look."

Tip #2: Role-play your verbal communication. More than clothing contributes to your overall personal image. Do you speak clearly, professionally, and at an appropriate pace and sound level when first meeting someone? Ask a friend to role-play and look for ways you can modify your verbal communication to create a better first impression.

Tip #3: Evaluate your nonverbal communication. Do you shake hands like a limp fish? Practice nonverbal communication, like shaking hands firmly and establishing good eye contact.

Tip #4: Examine your attitude. Do you smile when first meeting someone, even if you have other things on your mind? Are you focusing on that person and giving them your full attention? If not, you might be harming your image.

Tip #5: Scrutinize your grooming. Do your hair and makeup project the right image? Maybe it's time to consult a stylist to create a different look.

Taking this extra time to analyze and manage your image will greatly improve your odds of making a good first impression on hiring managers during those initial three to five seconds. Feeling good about what you're wearing and how you look will also help you project confidence during your interview.

Image and attire – my final advice

One final piece of advice about your image and attire: *It can be the reason you don't get the job, but it won't be the sole reason that you do.*

Your attire and the image you project to others is what I like to call the "icing on the cake." The most important aspect of getting a job isn't what you're wearing – it's what is in your head and in your heart. Hiring managers don't give job offers to the candidates who are the best dressed. They give job offers to those who are the most qualified and who exude passion and energy for the position.

If you are on a tight budget, head to consignment or thrift shops. You'll be able to find high-quality work attire at a fraction of the prices at high-end department stores. Consignment shops usually also have beautiful antique and gently worn contemporary jewelry that can add pizzazz to any outfit.

No matter what you decide to wear to your interview, make sure you've done all your other homework leading up to this step. Then walk into every interview prepared to show the hiring manager that you are the best person for the job, by demonstrating how you can contribute to the company and to the company's goals.

To choose the best possible outfit for your next interview, use the **Interview Attire Check List (page 281)** template in the **Appendix** (and online).

**CHAPTER 24
KEY TAKEAWAYS**

As the old saying goes: "Perception is reality." Think about the image you want to project during your job interview. Choose an outfit that portrays this image and is appropriate for the time of year, your geographic location, and the job, company, industry.

PART 7

ACE THE INTERVIEW

CHAPTER 25

NAVIGATE THE INTERVIEW DAY WITHOUT STRESS

One day I was sitting in my office on a conference call. I glanced up at the clock on the wall and saw there were about 25 minutes until I needed to conduct another interview for an open position in my department. Just then, a car pulled up outside the building, directly in front of my office windows.

While I sat at my desk finishing the conference call, I saw a woman primp for the next 20 minutes. She put on makeup and brushed and sprayed her hair while clouds of hair spray billowed from an open car window. Obviously nervous, she re-did her lipstick several times. Finally, she sat very still with her eyes closed and looked like she was giving herself an internal pep talk, meditating, or praying. Then she got out of her car and walked into the building.

Minutes later, the receptionist called to tell me my interview candidate had just arrived. I walked to the lobby and, sure enough, it was the same woman from the car. When she saw me and realized I'd been sitting in the office in front of her car, her face turned bright red. She was so embarrassed she could hardly say her name when I shook her hand and introduced myself. I had to give her credit for making sure she arrived early to the interview and for trying to look her best, but I could tell she was mortified.

Don't let your interview get derailed by little things like this. You've spent a lot of time on your job search creating your resume, updating your LinkedIn profile, preparing a list of references, obtaining recommendations, writing customized cover letters, and even conducting practice interviews. When the actual interview day arrives, ensure it goes as smoothly as possible by following these eight recommendations:

Know where you need to go. Don't wait until right before an interview to ensure you have the correct address and phone number. Verify these online by checking the company website a few days prior.

Download driving directions. Or, program the address into your smart phone or GPS to find out the potential routes and estimated drive times. I also like using Google Maps to zoom in and see what the actual building and surrounding area look like. If you're really unsure of where your interview is, drive there on the weekend so you can determine the best route and where to park *before* the big day. Don't rely on technology alone – always have a hard copy with the address and driving directions, just in case.

Obtain the correctly spelled name of the interviewer. And remember, bring a print out of the job posting. It always surprises me how many people show up and can't remember the name of the hiring manager or even the job title of the position for which they're interviewing. *Don't* be one of those people.

Schedule enough time for the interview. Block your calendar so you won't need to rush from one interview to the next, straight to another appointment, or back to work. If your discussion is going well, the interview might run late or you may be asked to interview with others. Make sure that if you're asked to stay longer to interview with other people or to fill out paperwork, you can do so.

Conduct a mirror check. Actually, do a double check. Do a head-to-toe mirror check once before leaving your house. Then, right before you get out of your car to walk in, take another quick look in the mirror. Hair in place? Check. Nothing stuck in between teeth? Check.

Pop a breath mint. While doing your second mirror check in the car, chew on a breath mint and finish it before your interview. Never, ever chew gum or walk in carrying a cup of coffee.

Turn off your cell phone. Yes, OFF, not put it on vibrate mode. That is because almost everyone can hear a cell phone vibrating wildly in a purse, briefcase, or pocket. Your concentration should be on the hiring manager, not your phone.

Take a bathroom break before the interview. Use the restroom before you leave your house and avoid too much coffee or other liquids shortly before your interview. If you need to use a bathroom when you arrive at the company, ask the receptionist to point you to them *before* he or she informs the hiring manager that you've arrived.

If you're wondering about the woman I saw primping in front of my office windows – I gave her the job. After we sat down for the interview she apologized for what I had seen through the windows. She explained how she was so excited about the job opportunity that when she arrived early, she had touched up her hair and makeup to help ease her jitters. Then she laughed about the odds of parking directly outside the office of the hiring manager. Her honesty was refreshing, and she was able to overcome her initial embarrassment through her sense of humor and strong communication skills.

After the interview, I also obtained feedback on the candidate from the receptionist – who told me the woman I'd just interviewed had been one of the nicest and most professionally behaved candidates with whom she'd ever spoken. When it comes to the day of your job interview, remember that you are "on stage" from the moment you pull into the company's parking lot until after the interview when you are leaving the parking lot. This means don't use your cell phone or talk to anyone about your interview until you have left the employer's offices and are on your way home or to a coffee shop – you never know who might overhear your conversation. Also, be polite and professional to EVERYONE because you never know who will report back to the hiring manager with feedback on their encounter with you.

Positive internal dialog – give yourself a pep talk

I mentioned earlier in this chapter how I could see the candidate in her car through my office windows. Right before she got out of her vehicle, she sat very still with her eyes closed and it looked like she was giving herself an internal pep talk, meditating, or praying. This can actually have a very powerful effect on your job interview.

If you followed the process in this book, then the night before your job interview, you fell asleep while envisioning yourself having a successful meeting with the hiring manager or recruiter. It can also be helpful to give yourself a pep talk right before your interview. On the day of the interview, either before you leave home or before you walk into your interview, mentally remind yourself of all the things you'll do, for example:

"I am going to pay careful attention to everything I notice about the company, the hiring manager, and the topics we discuss. I'm going to sell my skills and myself during the interview, but I will also take the time to find out if the job is a good fit for me. I will have fun during this interview and if this is the right job for me, then I will be offered the position."

Determine your own internal dialog, based on your situation. Just know that proactively giving yourself a pep talk and defining your objectives for the interview will help you manifest your goals into reality.

As you prepare for your interview, use the **Interview Preparation Check List (page 282)** template in the **Appendix** (and online) to ensure you don't forget anything important.

CHAPTER 25
KEY TAKEAWAYS

Job interviews can be challenging. To navigate the day with the least amount of stress, take time to properly prepare, like knowing where you need to go, blocking out enough time in your schedule, ensuring you're ready from head-to-toe before meeting the hiring manager, and giving yourself a quick pep talk.

DON'T FORGET TO INTERVIEW THE COMPANY AND HIRING MANAGER

We've touched on this briefly throughout the book, but most job candidates seem to think job interviews are solely about proving that they are the best fit for an open position. Having spent many years of my career on the other side of the table as a hiring manager, I will say it's actually a two-way street. A job seeker must also make sure the company and manager will be a good fit for them. Are you interviewing the company? If not, it's time you started.

Going into an interview realizing that you (the job seeker) also need to make sure the company and hiring manager will be a good fit for you, can help reduce some of the typical interview jitters and nervousness. Why? Because it requires you to focus on observing the company and the hiring manager, which aids in keeping your emotions in check and forces you to think rationally about what you're seeing and hearing. Here is what I mean:

Take note of your surroundings. From the time you arrive in the parking lot, take notes mentally in your head of what you see and hear. What does the office space look like? Is it clean and neat? Is it formal or casual in appearance? Are the receptionist and other employees friendly and immediately helpful?

Observe the inside of the company. Once you're inside, take a look at the office environment. Do employees look happy and hardworking? How are employees dressed – casually or in formal business attire? Is the work environment open cubicles or workspaces or is it mainly offices with doors? Is the office space quiet or fairly loud?

Observe the hiring manager. Is he or she prepared for your interview? How do they act when they greet you? If they walk you from the lobby to their office or to a conference room, how do they behave when passing other employees on the way there? Is the hiring manager organized with a list of questions to ask? Do they have your resume and the job description printed out with notes written in the margins? Can you picture yourself working for this person or does it conjure up mental images of sheer horror?

Kelly had twice previously accepted jobs that turned out to be a poor fit and had made her professional life fairly miserable. *Her problem?* Kelly had seen her job interviews as a one-way street and hadn't been interviewing the company and hiring manager. Because of this, Kelly had accepted jobs at companies that were much too formal and rigid for her personal style.

The solution? After she began practicing this technique, she was better able to evaluate each company's culture and the hiring manager's style during job interviews, and ended up finding a job at a company that was a much better fit.

To help you successfully evaluate a company and hiring manager, go somewhere right after the interview, like a nearby coffee shop, and think about your answers to the following questions:

- What did you observe about the office?
- What did you observe about the people you met?
- Based on what you saw and heard, how would you describe the company culture?
- What did you observe about the hiring manager?
- What were some of the questions the hiring manager asked?
- Does your personal style fit in with the company and hiring manager's style?
- Are there any issues that came up during the discussion or potential issues that stand out as you think about the company and hiring manager?
- Can you picture yourself working at this company? Working for this manager?

Reviewing your answers to these questions should give you a much better idea whether or not the company and hiring manager would be a good fit for your personal style and with what you want to accomplish in your career. Taking this time for evaluation will help you make better choices as you consider your job opportunities.

Use the following **Appendix** template at the back of this book (and online) to help you evaluate the company and hiring manager:

- **Interview Follow-Up Notes (page 283)**

CHAPTER 26
KEY TAKEAWAYS

A job interview shouldn't be a one-way street. In addition to selling yourself to the hiring manager, don't forget to interview the company and hiring manager to help determine if the job, company culture, and style of the hiring manager will be a good fit for you.

TREAT TELEPHONE INTERVIEWS LIKE IN-PERSON INTERVIEWS

Some of the worst interviews I've experienced as a hiring manager were telephone interviews. I once had a job seeker, Daniel, take my telephone interview while driving. I could hear everything, from the traffic noise to ambulance sirens to Daniel's stop at a service station to fill his car with gas. He could have simply sat inside his parked car for the duration of the call. Instead, he wrongly assumed I wouldn't notice that he took the call while on the road.

What does this tell me as a hiring manager? Unfortunately, that he thought the job was unimportant. This lackadaisical attitude also came through in several of his interview answers, which further confirmed his questionable character. As you're probably guessing, he didn't get the job.

Michelle was another candidate who didn't get the job after our telephone interview. I scheduled the interview at a time Michelle specifically requested, and doing so forced me to reschedule an internal meeting. The moment I called Michelle, I could tell it wasn't going to be a smooth interview. She answered the telephone with small children screaming in the background. The noise was so loud she had to ask twice who was calling.

When I asked if we should reschedule our appointment to a more convenient time for her to talk, Michelle responded, *"Oh, it's always like this, so now's as good a time as any."* I tried to make the best of the situation and began asking questions from my pre-written list. Unfortunately, I could barely hear Michelle's responses over the noise in the house. Multiple times I had to ask her to repeat her comments.

A few minutes into the telephone interview, I could tell from the tone of her voice that Michelle was getting frustrated with the background noise when she began asking me to repeat my questions. That is when I was forced to end the interview. It's not that I don't love children, I do. I have three wonderful daughters and lots of nieces and nephews, but a hiring manager can't conduct an interview when she can't hear the candidate

In an interesting twist, noise can sometimes be what breaks the ice during an interview. My telephone interview with Paul was off to a good start. His resume showed me he was qualified for the job and his explanations and stories confirmed his grasp on the important aspects of the position. Then I heard a loud dog bark. Not lots of barking. Just the very loud and annoyed sounding, "Woof!" of a large dog.

Paul apologized. *"I drove to my apartment so I could do this interview from my home office where it would be quiet. I'm not usually here at this time of the day and my dog, Rascal, seems to think it's after work, and time for us to play outside."* Then Paul laughed. *"He just brought me his toy ball and dropped it at my feet to let me know he wants to go outside."*

We both laughed and continued with the interview. But a few minutes later I heard a loud noise and what sounded like the telephone falling onto the desk. Rascal apparently didn't like being ignored and jumped onto Paul's desk, sending everything on it flying onto the floor. Paul was laughing hard when he picked the phone back up, explained what had just happened, and asked if he could call me back in five minutes.

When Paul called me back in exactly five minutes, he was still laughing. He got Rascal off his desk, took him outside and played catch a few times, and then put his desk back to normal. Rascal remained curled up at his feet and quiet for the rest of our interview. A few days later when Paul arrived at my office for the in-person interview, we had a good laugh about how Rascal lived up to his name.

As a hiring manager, a situation like Paul's doesn't bother me very much. It actually allows me to learn a lot about a candidate in a short amount of time. For example, Paul took the time to drive home to be in a quiet and confidential location for the telephone interview (with the exception of Rascal's abnormal behavior). I could tell from our discussion that Paul had his resume on the desk in front of him as well as a print out of the job description. I could also hear him writing notes during the interview. When it came time for Paul to ask me questions, I heard him flip to a list of questions he had obviously pre-written.

Paul also handled Rascal's bad dog behavior without getting upset and with a sense of humor. He assessed the situation and immediately understood what he needed to do to get the interview back on track – take Rascal outside for a few minutes of play and then get his paperwork straightened out and back on his desk. This behavior showed me that Paul likely remained calm and logical in stressful situations.

Sometimes, no matter how hard you prepare for a telephone interview, something unexpected will happen. How you handle these situations will make you stand out from other candidates. Whether you stand out in a good or negative way is up to you.

For many jobs, the first step in the interview process is a telephone interview (also called a "phone screen"), so don't discount the importance of it. Here is how you can ace your next one:

Treat telephone and in-person interviews the same way. Follow all the steps in this book and treat telephone interviews seriously. Research the company and industry, prepare potential interview questions and answers, and practice interviewing over the telephone with someone so you can get the feel for it before the actual interview.

Practice your telephone voice. Practice your telephone voice so you speak clearly and at the right volume. Introduce yourself using a strong, confident voice. Avoid rambling and speaking in a monotone way. Hiring managers want to hear your passion for the job, so try smiling while you talk. This will help you sound happy and positive. Feeling a little lethargic? Try standing up when you answer a question to sound more energetic.

Eliminate background noise and interference for the interview. Ensure you can conduct the interview in peace and quiet. Solicit your family's help to reduce or eliminate noise while you're being interviewed. If you're interviewing from your home, be sure no one will pick up one of the other telephone lines and accidentally interrupt the call. Turn cell phones off. The same goes for the TV or stereo – turn them all off. Put pets outside (or in the garage) with food and water or ask someone to watch them and keep them quiet. Ask a family member or friend to watch your children or take them to a park during your call.

Have all the right documents available. This includes your resume, the job description, your list of questions for the hiring manager, a note pad and several pens, reference list, recommendation letters – all of the documents you'd normally bring to an in-person interview. Put them on the desk or table in front of you and spread them out so you can easily see the information. It can also help to have quick access to the Internet, just in case it is needed.

Dress the part. There is something to be said for putting on the clothes you'd wear to an in-person interview and wearing them for your telephone interview. Just the act of getting dressed for the part will help your mind get ready. As one client commented, *"You were right. Looking professional helped me sound professional over the telephone, even though the hiring manager couldn't see me."*

Have something to drink nearby. You never know when your mouth will go dry, so have something close by to drink. Just don't accidentally knock it over onto all your paperwork. And, don't chew gum, eat food, or smoke while you're on the telephone call. Trust me, the interviewer will hear you.

Listen and think before you speak. Allow the hiring manager or HR person to take the lead. Listen carefully to each question and, if need be, write the question on your notepad so you won't forget. Answer each question succinctly and with what I call "sound bytes," meaning keep answers short and to the point.

Regularly "check in" with the interviewer. I once interviewed a candidate over the phone and his answers were so long-winded that he kept forgetting my questions. He would ramble on and on, get confused, then stop and ask, *"Oh, what was your question again?"* and then continue talking. So I started timing his answers. He averaged about five minutes per answer. For one question he talked for almost ten minutes without checking in with me to see if I had any questions or comments about what he had said. Don't let this happen to you. Keep your answers fairly short and every so often, check back in with the interviewer to make sure you remain on track:

"Would you like my overall philosophy on that topic or an example of how I'd handle that type of situation?"

"Are there any other questions you have for me regarding my experience in xyz?"

"That was an example of how I'd handle it as an employee. Would you also like an example of how I'd handle it from a management perspective?"

"Did that answer your question or would you like another example?"

Finish your telephone interview just like you would close an in-person interview. Use the techniques from Chapter 22 to close the telephone interview with class. Practice asking questions that will help you uncover what the hiring manager or HR representative thinks of your qualifications, the next steps in the hiring process, and if you'll advance to the in-person interview round. Reiterate your interest in the position and thank him or her for their time.

The Do's and Don'ts of telephone interviews

As you prepare for telephone interviews, here are a few more Do's and Don'ts to consider:

DO:

- Take a bathroom break *before* your telephone interview.
- Watch your body language because it can affect your energy level and the tone of your voice.
- Sound excited about the job opportunity.
- Use a headset (if you have one) so you can leave your hands free to take notes.
- Pause a few seconds before answering each question to ensure the interviewer is done speaking.
- Say thank you to the hiring manager at the end and send either an email or handwritten thank you note.

DON'T:

- Drive while interviewing.
- Use a speakerphone.

- Interrupt the interviewer.
- Be afraid of brief silent periods. Some candidates are so uncomfortable with silence, especially on the phone, that they try to fill every gap with comments. This will make you sound nervous.
- If you are on your home telephone and call waiting beeps, DON'T answer it. If you know the interviewer can hear the beeps, tell them it should end soon.

Tips for video interviews

Due to geographic location or to save time, some hiring managers conduct interviews using social media video tools such as Skype, Facetime, GoToMeeting, or Meeting Burner. Treat a video interview as seriously as you would an in-person interview using all the previously mentioned techniques. In addition, there are also a few technical items you'll want to work out ahead of time:

- Find the best location to set up the video and ensure nothing is behind you that could be distracting – you want the focus on you, not the crazy-looking picture on the wall or the stacks of dirty laundry.
- Test to ensure adequate lighting and sound.
- Determine the best place to sit so you're not too close, but not too far away from the camera.
- Look directly into the camera lens when responding to maintain good "eye contact" with the interviewer.
- Conduct a few practice video interviews with family members or friends and then make any necessary adjustments.

CHAPTER 27
KEY TAKEAWAYS

For many jobs, you must first get through a telephone interview before you're invited to an in-person interview, so don't discount the importance. Take them seriously by preparing in the same way you'd prepare for an in-person interview.

MODIFY YOUR COMMUNICATION STYLE FOR PANEL INTERVIEWS

A young woman I was mentoring called me with panic in her voice. The recruiter had just told her that her job interview had been changed from individual interviews to a panel interview. Due to time constraints, instead of meeting individually with the hiring manager and then with two other managers, she would now meet with them all at once in a 45-minute panel interview.

Jackie was worried, because she'd never been through a panel interview. The thought of sitting across from three people while they rapidly fired questions at her was terrifying.

Many companies are changing their hiring practices to bring others into the process, and due to time constraints, this often means holding panel interviews instead of individual job interviews. At some point in your career, just like Jackie, you'll most likely have to go through a panel interview.

To be successful in panel interviews, you'll want to slightly modify your preparation as well as your communication style. Here are 7 tips to consider:

Tip #1: Find out who will be on the interview panel. Ask the recruiter or hiring manager for the names and titles of everyone who will be on the panel. This will help you gain a better understanding of what will be important to each person. Are they in sales, service, marketing, operations, research and development, finance, process improvement, HR, etc.? What would your relationship be to each? Would he or she be a coworker or would you interact with them regularly, even though they're in a different department?

Tip #2: Brainstorm the questions each person might ask. Based on their role in the company, think through the types of questions they might ask you during the interview. For example, if you are interviewing for a job as a marketing manager and you find out that one person on the panel is a sales manager, figure out the types of questions he or she might ask, such as: When you create a promotional program, what is your process to ensure it will be successful with the sales teams? What are some of the issues you've encountered while working with sales teams and how have you overcome them? Then, practice your answers.

Tip #3: Introduce yourself to each person. When you show up for the panel interview, approach each person and introduce yourself while shaking his or her hand. Ask for a business card from everyone, so you can place these in front of you in the order in which they're sitting. If they don't have business cards with them, write down their names on a piece of paper (in the order in which they're sitting) and have this in front of you during the interview. That way, you'll know who you are addressing as you answer questions.

Tip #4: Modify your communication style. In an individual interview, you would respond to questions by answering the person directly. But in a panel interview, you need to be careful not to exclude the rest of the panel during your comments. Make eye contact with the person asking the question and begin by directing your answer to him or her. Then, look at the other panel members as you finish the rest of your comments, so each person feels included in the conversation. At the very end of your answer, look back at the person who asked you the question, just in case they have a follow-up question.

Tip #5: Demonstrate that you're making connections during the conversation. Instead of just answering each person's question, see if you can make connections and demonstrate your active listening skills. Let's say that one panel member asked you to walk them through your process for creating a successful promotional program. Then, a little while later, someone asks you to *"Tell me about a time when something went wrong with a promotion you were running."* You could refer back to your other answer by saying something like: *"Joe, when you asked me to walk you through my process for creating a promotional program, one of the key steps I mentioned was to obtain feedback from the sales team and test the program from beginning to end with several members. Early in* *my career, I didn't realize the importance of obtaining feedback before rolling out a new sales promotion. I once tried to…"* then tell how you didn't include that step, what happened, and what you learned from your mistake.

Tip #6: Modify how you ask questions at the end of the interview. Just like you would prepare for an individual interview, bring your list of potential questions to ask at the end of the interview. Try to relate a few of your questions back to what was discussed during the panel interview. For example, if one of the interviewers asked what you know about the company's key competitors, you might relate back to that with one of your own questions, such as: *"I know we discussed some of the company's main competitors, but I'm curious to know what each of you sees as the biggest threat to the growth of the company. Is it a competitor, or is it something else?"* Also, because it is a panel interview, don't be surprised if time runs out and you aren't given the opportunity to ask any questions.

Tip #7: Follow-up with each person. As I've mentioned, following up after a job interview with a thank you note can be a good way to differentiate yourself from other candidates. In the case of a panel interview, you should send a personalized thank you note or email to each member of the interview panel.

At first, a panel job interview might sound intimidating. But with the right prep work and by modifying your communication style during the interview, you'll be able to increase your chances for a successful interview.

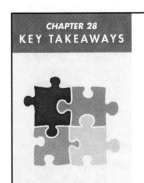

CHAPTER 28
KEY TAKEAWAYS

Don't be intimidated if you're told you'll be in a panel interview with several managers. Conduct research to find out information about the participants, think through questions each person might ask, modify your communication style to incorporate everyone during your answers, and don't forget to follow up with a thank you note or email to each participant.

PART 8

AFTER THE INTERVIEW

DO THIS, AFTER THE INTERVIEW

You've made it through the job interview. You've written down your observations about the company and hiring manager so you can evaluate them. Now it's time to remember key information and next steps.

I always recommend going to a coffee shop immediately after an interview to write notes. That's because we humans are fallible and tend to forget things fairly quickly. Most studies have shown that people will forget up to 75% of what they learned within one or two days. The faster you write down everything from the interview, the more accurate the information will be.

So order that vanilla soy iced latte or caramel macchiato (can you tell I'm from Seattle?) and write down what you can remember, such as:

- The documents you provided the hiring manager (or HR rep) during or right after the interview.
- Issues that came up during the discussion.
- Questions you stumbled on or felt you could have answered better.
- Additional documents or pieces of information the hiring manager asked you to provide (ones you didn't have with you and you'll need to send or email later).

Next, use what you learned from this interview to improve your skills and prepare for the next one. Ask yourself:

- What went well during my interview?
- What didn't go as well as I'd hoped?
- If I could do the interview again, what would I do differently?

For example, one client realized the caffeine from her morning coffee made her nervous and fidgety and negatively impacted her ability to interview well. Another realized she tended to ramble and needed to provide more concise answers when asked questions such as, *"Tell me about a time when you..."*

The key is to unemotionally and very logically look at what happened – don't beat yourself up if an interview didn't go as well as you had hoped or expected. Don't criticize yourself about how horrible you did or how awful some of your answers might have sounded. Suck it up, put your pride and ego into a closet, and shut the door. Then take a step back from the situation and analyze your interview. Go back through it several times in your head and write down everything you can think of related to what went well and what didn't. Then use this information to make changes before your next job interview. Changes might include:

- Updating your resume.
- Modifying cover letters.
- Obtaining more or different references or recommendations.
- Modifying your answers to interview questions.
- Spending additional time in mock interviews to polish your skills.
- Creating a portfolio of work examples.
- Bringing more copies of your resume to job interviews.
- Choosing different interview attire.
- Conducting additional research on the company or industry.

Remember, everything in life is about learning and experiencing. The best gift you can give yourself is to slow down enough to realize what you've seen, heard, and observed so you can use that information to improve for the future. Taking the time to look at what went well and what didn't will make you wiser for your next interview.

Say "thank you" the right way

As she walked out of the office building where she'd just finished a job interview, Kate wanted to jump in the air and dance across the street. And it wasn't because the sun was finally shining in Seattle. Her interview had gone so well that Kate was sure they'd offer her the job. Or so she thought. Unfortunately, Kate didn't bother to follow-up after the interview with a thank you note.

Right after you jot down your notes from the interview, it's time to thank your interviewer for his or her time. And just for the record, no, the thank you note is *not* dead. It is actually a great way to reiterate your interest in the position and demonstrate your follow-through skills because it can signify the level of service you'll provide clients or customers, if you're offered the job.

Some job seekers believe their work is done as soon as the interview is over. But following up after an interview can make the difference in whether or not you're the candidate chosen for the job. How you follow up after an interview depends mainly on the culture of the company. Typically, this means sending a thank you email later that same day. A thank you email is usually appropriate for companies in the high-tech or computer industry.

If the company culture is more formal/traditional (banks and financial companies, government) or customer service focused (retail, healthcare) a handwritten or typed and mailed thank you note sent within 24 hours is still acceptable and often preferred. Use your best judgment to determine if you should send a thank you email or a handwritten note, based on your company and industry research.

A thank you phone call is *not* something I recommend. Speaking from many years experience as a hiring manager, the last thing I wanted was a candidate interrupting my busy day to thank me for the job interview they just had.

Don't text thank you notes either – a hiring manager will hate this. Thankfully, I've only had this happen once, when a candidate texted, "Thx for the intrvw!" While sending a text might be convenient, it is not appropriate for thank you notes.

Include the right information

Not sure what to include in your thank you note to the hiring manager? Here are my recommendations:

- The hiring manager's name
- The title of the open position for which you just interviewed
- Something specific about the interview or an important item that was discussed
- Your interest in the position

- Your appreciation for their time (the "thank you" part)
- Your recognition of the next steps in the hiring process
- Your contact information

Still unsure of what to write? Here is an example:

Dear <insert hiring manager's name>

Thank you for your time today to discuss the open position in your department, Customer Call Center Manager, Job ID #2727. Both the interview and the tour of the call center made for an exciting visit. I was impressed with the teamwork and positive spirit among the employees I met.

Your description of a "day in the life" of the manager position helped me gain a better understanding of the daily job responsibilities, and I appreciate your openness in sharing your key goals for the department. I'm excited about the possibility of using my call center background, specifically my expertise in process improvement and people management, to help you achieve the department objectives. The interview reinforced my interest in becoming a part of your team.

I look forward to hearing from you next week after you've interviewed the remaining two candidates. Thank you again for the opportunity to interview for the Customer Call Center Manager position. Should you have any additional questions, I may be reached at (222) 222-2222 or Name.Name@TBD.com.

Sincerely,

Your name here

Over the years, various studies have shown that hiring managers are less likely to hire a candidate if they don't send a thank you note after an interview. This is because it can demonstrate a lack of follow-through skills or that the candidate isn't serious about the job opportunity. Don't be like Kate – take the time to send a customized thank you note or email to differentiate yourself from other candidates and to reinforce your interest in the position.

Create a follow up plan

In addition to sending a thank you note after your interview, it is also important to create your follow up plan. Because you've already learned how to close an interview with class (Chapter 22), you'll have asked the hiring manager about his or her next steps in the hiring process and the time frame for the hiring decision. Use this information to make a note in your calendar on the day you expect to hear back from the employer.

If you haven't heard anything within about two or three days after the hiring decision was to have been made, send a thoughtfully worded email to the hiring manager, reiterating your interest in the position and checking in on his or her progress in the hiring process. If you were working with a recruiter or someone in HR, it is best to first send a follow-up email directly to them (before you attempt to contact the hiring manager). Just know that things in a company can change quickly. Sometimes hiring managers end up interviewing more candidates than originally expected, which can extend the time it takes to fill the job. Other times budgets may be frozen, which can put the open position into a holding pattern. In the worst-case scenario, a budget may get unexpectedly cut, eliminating the previously available job.

If you haven't received a response to your check-in email within a few days, follow up with your network of contacts working at that company to see if they can (subtly) find out the status of the hiring process. This is easy to do, by asking a simple question of an employee who works in that department, or by asking the hiring manager (if your contact knows him/her):

Example 1: One of your network contacts might see an employee they know who works in the department for which you interviewed. He or she might say, *"Hi Joe! I'm glad I ran into you. I was wondering if there's still an open position in your department."* The employee's response will, hopefully, give you your answer on the status of the hiring process.

Example 2: One of your network contacts might see the hiring manager while standing in the line at the company cafeteria, after a meeting or walking in the hall and say, *"Hi Ann! I haven't seen you in a while. How have you been?'* And then after some initial chitchat asks, *"How is it going filling that open position in your department?"*

If the hiring manager tells your contact that she or he has just filled the position or that the new person begins next week, then you'll know that you didn't get the job. You can also check the company's online listing of open job postings. If the position for which you applied and interviewed is no longer posted, that is a sign that the position has been filled. If you choose to ask anyone in your network for help in finding out the status of the job, always be polite and respectful of their time and thank them for their help. If you still don't know the status after these efforts, call the HR person and attempt to speak with them over the telephone to find out the status of the job.

If you don't hear back - move up the chain of command

Let's say none of those follow up tactics work. That's when it is time to move up the chain of command. For example, if you were working with a recruiter or someone in HR and you haven't received a response to your check-in email or telephone call after several more days, send an email directly to the hiring manager. Again, be polite and professional in your attempt to find out the progress of the hiring process.

If your email attempts at following up don't elicit any response, your final option is to call the person directly – just be prepared with what you'll say, be it live or in case you need to leave a voicemail message.

Unfortunately, not every employer treats job candidates with due respect by notifying all those who went through the interview process after a hiring decision has been made. In my mind, this is a required step, and as a hiring manager, I personally called all candidates who made it to the final round of in-person interviews after I had made my decision.

Working as an executive coach to managers, I've heard just about every possible excuse as to why they don't have the time or don't bother to notify candidates who are not chosen for job openings. And I always call "bull" on all of their excuses. There is no legitimate reason why a manager can't take the time to make five to ten quick telephone calls – as there should never be more than that number of candidates in the final round of in-person interviews.

When you don't hear back after both email and telephone follow up, you should move on to other job opportunities and think about what you've learned about that employer:

- Do you really want to work for a manager who doesn't take the time to notify job candidates after a decision has been made?

- If you were working with a recruiter or someone in HR during the process, do you want to work for a company where HR thinks so little of human assets that they don't keep potential employees updated on their hiring progress?
- How you were treated during the process and afterwards could be a reflection of the company's overall culture – is that how you'd want to be treated as an employee if you worked there?

My same advice holds true if you've applied for several different positions at one employer and either haven't heard back or you've gone on interviews and then never received any closure. Take a step back, take a deep breath, and think through if that is the kind of company you want to work for. Remember, interviewing is a two-way street. The employer is trying to find the candidate who is the best fit for the job, but it is *your* responsibility to see if the hiring manager, department, and company are a good fit for *you*.

Employers who care about their employees know that their most important and valuable assets go home every night, and they have hiring processes that treat candidates with dignity and respect. This includes providing closure to all in-person interview candidates who are not chosen at the end of the hiring process. Throughout your job search efforts, look for employers whose values and behavior are in sync with yours.

**CHAPTER 29
KEY TAKEAWAYS**

Your work isn't over once you finish the job interview. Take time to jot down notes from your discussion with the hiring manager, analyze the interview, and send a thank you note. Then, create your follow up plan to ensure you stay informed on the progress of the hiring process. And never, ever pin all your hopes on one offer – continue pursuing all potential opportunities until you accept a job.

STAY ORGANIZED DURING YOUR JOB SEARCH

When I first met with Alicia her briefcase was overflowing with odds and ends of various paperwork. As we talked about her job search, it became clear that she was overwhelmed. Alicia had been sending her resume to any and every company and posting it on any online job board she could find. When she had received a recent call back, she had to ask the person to repeat their name and the name of the company – because she hadn't remembered that she had applied for a position at that employer. *Alicia's problem?* She wasn't taking the time to research and target specific job opportunities and then track the progress of each position.

I asked Alicia the following questions: *To what companies and positions have you already applied? For each of those, what information did you submit and on what date did you submit it? How did you submit it (electronic upload, email, or via mail delivery)? What is your next step for each job opportunity?* As I asked Alicia my questions, she became more and more horrified because she realized she didn't have the answers.

If you don't stay organized during your job search, the process can begin to spin out of control – as Alicia found out. And if you're wallpapering the world with your resume, then you probably aren't customizing your resume to each job opportunity or following the rest of the steps I've outlined in this book – steps that will increase your chances of finding a job that is a good fit.

Here is the process I tell my clients to follow so they can proactively keep everything straight and simplify their job search process:

- Purchase folders and create one folder for each job for which you apply.
- Label the folder with the name of the company and the job title.

- As you begin doing the prep work we've discussed for each job, place the hard copy print outs of everything in the folder, such as the job description, research about the company and industry, your filled out job requirements analysis document, your customized resume, etc.

- When you submit information or apply online, write down the specific items you provided, how you submitted them, the next steps you'll take to follow up, and then print out a copy of everything you submitted – add all of this to your file folder.

- Create a tracking document (or use the **Job Search Tracking Log (page 284)** located in the **Appendix**) so you can track all of your job search efforts.

- Keep your job search folders in one location where you'll have easy access to them.

- Never type over information in your existing resume. Always perform a "Save As" function and rename your document with your name, job, employer, and the new date. You'll want to save each version of your resume, just in case you get called for an in-person interview and need to bring the same version you submitted.

- Some people also like to keep an electronic file with all of their job search information, with one electronic folder for every job opportunity (just like you would do in hard copy). Make sure you back up your computer on a regular basis to ensure you never lose any of your information.

Alicia had been sending out her resume to all kinds of companies for all types of jobs because she thought that the more resumes she sent out, the better chance she'd have of getting a call back from someone. Many people have this same thought process – that sending out more resumes means more job opportunities. This is rarely the case. What usually happens is they waste precious time spinning their wheels applying for too many jobs and positions that don't actually fit their background or career goals. That is what happened with Alicia. She'd been wasting a lot of time and energy applying for jobs that weren't a good fit and that she wasn't even excited about.

After working through these steps with Alicia, she began feeling much more organized in her job search. But as I taught her the job seeking basics I've explained in this book, she became frustrated because she felt I was slowing down her process. I asked Alicia to trust me and to trust in the process of working through these fundamental steps. We took the time to define her career aspirations and then chose a handful of jobs that really appealed to her. We followed the process in this book of researching those jobs and companies, and then conducted a S.W.O.T. analysis (Chapter 7) so Alicia could see how she stacked up against the job requirements.

Two weeks after we rewrote her resume and updated her LinkedIn profile, recruiters began proactively contacting Alicia. She was completely shocked – this had never happened. It changed her perspective and helped her see that taking a step back and getting strategic in her job search process actually saved her time and got her better (and more) results than her previous approach.

As you work your way through the job search process, pursue the opportunities you really want and that are the best for you given your strengths, weaknesses, and career goals. Handle your search wisely, prioritizing your time and spending it on identifying the right jobs at the companies where you'd most like to work. Use your time to pursue the five *right* jobs, not 100 *wrong* ones. Then, stay organized by keeping track of what you've done and your next steps for each opportunity.

Use the **Job Search Tracking Log (page 284)** from the **Appendix** templates at the back of this book (and online) to help you stay organized throughout your job search process.

CHAPTER 30
KEY TAKEAWAYS

To keep from feeling overwhelmed in the job search process, stay organized. Keep track of the jobs you apply to, what you submit, how you submit it and when, as well as your next steps. Prioritize your time and apply to only a handful of jobs at the companies where you would most like to work.

AVOID GIVING AWAY YOUR JOB SEARCH

Most companies require that your manager be notified when you apply for a position in a different department *within* the company. This is to help ensure that managers work together and that no workload or productivity issues are created when an employee moves to a different department. It also helps prevent "problem employees" from hopping from one department to another to avoid being discovered. So if you're seeking a new position within your current company, it is unlikely you'll be able to disguise your job search.

If you're looking for a position *outside* of your current company, it is wise to disguise your job search. Why? There are some managers who may end your employment if your search is discovered. Or in other cases, it can sour the relationship with your boss, which can be detrimental if you change your mind about finding a new job.

Most companies also have policies against employees using the Internet during work hours, unless conducting research is part of their job responsibilities. Getting caught using the Internet for personal reasons could result in reprimands, written warnings, or even dismissal – not something you want while you are job hunting, especially if you economically need that job until you land another one.

Hiding your job search can be difficult in the era of social media, so think before you act when posting online or discussing your search with others (especially coworkers). Here are tips to avoid giving away your job search:

Keep profiles updated. Always keep online social media profiles up-to-date. You won't trigger suspicions when you're actively looking for a new job because people will think you're being diligent about keeping your information current – as always! I joke with my clients that it's similar to neighbors thinking you're about to sell your house the minute you start improving your front yard, because you've never done it.

Lie low electronically. Unless you currently don't have a job or are working for yourself, avoid posting in social media about your job search. You may think your profiles are completely private, but you would be surprised by how many employers find out about job searches this way.

Be careful what you display online. If you join online groups for job hunting, make sure they are hidden from public view. For example, on LinkedIn you can change your Group settings so certain groups you've joined aren't visible on your public profile.

Don't wallpaper the world with your resume. As I shared in the last chapter, uploading your resume to every possible job board usually doesn't get you the job you desire – contrary to what many think. Even worse, you could get unwanted views from your current company's HR recruiters or your boss. Instead, take the time to conduct research and target your resume to only those few key jobs you really want.

Conduct your job search from home, not work. Never use company equipment like a computer or cell phone for your job search. These leave electronic footprints that can be traced back to you. Further, coworkers can easily overhear your telephone conversations in a cubicle environment and even see your computer screen, which can give away your job search and cause it to spread like wildfire throughout the company. Always use a personal computer and phone. Don't have a computer? Use the computers at your local library or ask to borrow one from a family member or friend. If you graduated from a nearby college, you can also check for availability of computers in the college's computer lab. Some churches and local organizations also provide computer access for job seekers.

Conduct job hunting on your own time. Never job search on company time. Using paid time for personal endeavors is the same as stealing from the company. Take a personal or vacation day for job search work, telephone interviews, and in-person interviews.

Choose appropriate times for telephone interviews. Preferably, schedule telephone interviews before work, during lunch, or right after work. Even better, schedule them for your day off. Avoid telephone interviews during lunch hours, unless you drive home for them or have a personal cell phone and a quiet location where you can speak in confidence. Most hiring managers understand that if they're interviewing someone already employed, they'll need to work around that person's schedule.

Further, most savvy hiring managers look for potential employees who specifically state that their telephone interview needs to be scheduled at a time that won't conflict with their existing job, so they won't break any company policies. As a hiring manager, a red flag is raised in my mind about the ethics of any candidate who is willing to use company time for their interview.

Be careful whom you tell. Not everyone at work is your friend and can keep information confidential. A client had once confidentially shared with a coworker that she was looking for another job. She thought this person was her friend. The next day my client's boss confronted her about her job search. It turns out the coworker was the person who shared the confidential information with others within the company and had purposely started rumors so she could get her in trouble with their manager.

In addition to keeping your job search a secret, it's incredibly important to manage your time wisely. Conducting a job search while employed requires excellent time management skills because the majority of work must be done in the evenings and on weekends. To stay organized, motivated, and on-track, write down a list of the goals you want to accomplish each week and schedule time for completion. For example, your list might include, "Update resume on Saturday, have John and Mary review my resume and provide feedback on Sunday/Monday, update LinkedIn profile on Tuesday evening, brainstorm list of references on Wednesday evening, begin contacting potential references on Thursday evening, research targeted companies on Saturday…"

Trying to maintain a high level of productivity and performance quality in your current position while looking for a different job can also increase your stress level. Some clients have even felt like job searching required too much work and wasn't worth it. To keep stress at a manageable level, schedule some time off every week to simply relax and unwind – even if it is only for a few hours to read a book or go for a run in the park. Scheduling this down time into your life is one of the best ways to ensure you'll never feel too frazzled.

**CHAPTER 31
KEY TAKEAWAYS**

It is wise to avoid giving away your job search, especially if you are currently employed and looking for a position *outside* your existing company. Hiding your job search can be difficult in the era of social media, so think before you post anything online or discuss your search with others, especially coworkers.

CHAPTER 32

DON'T GET DISCOURAGED

Looking for a new job or switching careers isn't easy. But it can be accomplished a lot faster if you maintain a positive attitude and a "can do" spirit. *"No matter how frustrated I get while I'm conducting research online or applying for jobs, I keep telling myself to hang in there. That I can do this if I stay focused,"* my client Melanie told me during one of our sessions.

That little voice we hear in our heads before, during, or after situations throughout each day is known as 'self-talk.' This internal voice can be positive (like Melanie's) or negative. Either way, it often turns into a self-fulfilling prophecy.

For example, I often have people ask for advice on how to find a job or obtain a promotion. Those with a positive attitude – who believe they are worthy of finding their dream job or getting a promotion – are much more likely to accomplish their goal because their self-talk is positive. Their internal discussions reinforce their belief that they can figure out how to make it happen thus it becomes a self-fulfilling prophecy. And, their outlook on life tends to be optimistic.

On the flip side, people seeking a new job, a raise, or a promotion who have a poor attitude and doubt their ability to get hired or obtain the raise or promotion they want are engaging in negative self-talk. This internal negativity often leads to de-motivation and not wanting to take the steps needed to accomplish career goals. These people usually take much longer to find a job or never end up obtaining that coveted raise or promotion.

This is mainly because negative self-talk gives a person a reason to cut themselves slack, to be "off the hook" for their behavior and the results of their efforts (or lack thereof). How many times have you heard someone say something like, *"Oh, I'm not even going to apply for the job because they'll just give it to Jane (or John) anyway and then tell me I'm not qualified."*

Just like in the children's book, *The Little Engine That Could*, if you're getting frustrated in your job search, it is probably time to give yourself a few encouraging words. Mentally telling yourself, *"I think I can, I think I can,"* just might give you the motivation to continue moving forward.

Is your job search aimed at the right level?

Patricia was a client who lost her job in operations management when her employer downsized. She was frustrated with her job search because she hadn't received any job offers and several hiring managers told her she was over-qualified. *Patricia's problem?* She was aiming too low in her job search.

As a career coach, I've found that many people tend to shoot low in their job search when:

- They were laid off or fired and are of the mindset that they need to find a new job as quickly as possible due to their economic situation.
- They lack internal confidence about their skills and experience and end up targeting positions for which they're overqualified.
- They don't have a clear understanding of their strengths, weaknesses, and differentiators.
- They don't have a clearly defined job seeking plan.

Unfortunately, there are some potential dangers in aiming too low in your job search. One is a financial danger. Think of it this way, if you shoot too low and accept a job that pays $10,000 less per year than what you're actually worth, over the next 20 years it means you'll earn $200,000 less than if you'd taken the time to find a job that was a better fit for your skill set.

Other dangers are to your professional growth and personal well-being. By taking a job beneath your skill set, you'll be less likely to do work that allows you to grow and develop your abilities. This can quickly cause boredom, which can then lead to decreased productivity and even depression. Almost every person I know who accepted a position beneath their skill set ended up frustrated within his or her first six months on the job. That boredom and frustration can also cause increased stress, which can negatively impact almost all areas of life, even physical health.

Tips to avoid aiming too low in your job search

Here is how you can make sure you're not aiming too low in your job search:

Clearly define your job seeking goals. Use this book to map out your job search game plan to help you target the right positions. Someone once said, *"Hope is not a strategy."* Don't trust your next job (or your career) to luck or fate. Create your plan and stick to it – this will help ensure you won't deviate from your career objectives by looking at the wrong types of jobs during your search.

Know your strengths and weaknesses. Use the personal S.W.O.T. analysis (Chapter 7) to think of yourself as a competitive product with features, benefits, assets, and liabilities – a product to be marketed and improved year after year. Analyze your strengths and weaknesses so when you search for jobs, you can avoid targeting positions that are too far beneath your skills.

Determine your differentiators. Just as products have strengths that set them apart, so do people. Identify the things you do better than others. These are the things that will set you apart from other candidates and that make you special. Understanding your unique capabilities will keep you from accepting positions beneath your abilities.

Don't target being a 100% fit for a position. As a hiring manager, I never want to hire a candidate who is a 100% fit with the job requirements. Why? Because I know the person would quickly get bored. I always look for people who are about an 80% fit and who have an incredible drive for growth and personal development. These are the people who will be happier and more motivated employees.

Find mentors to help you keep a clear head. Look for people you admire and seek them out as mentors during your job search process. Use them to discuss potential positions and obtain their feedback. It can be helpful having unbiased opinions because the job search process can be an emotional journey.

After helping Patricia work through all the topics in this book, she realized she had been underselling her capabilities. Strengthened by this knowledge, she found open positions that were more suited to her skills and experience. We updated and repositioned her resume and LinkedIn profile to better showcase her strengths and unique differentiators. We also key worded them to better match the targeted jobs. And guess what? Within two months, Patricia received a job offer for one of her preferred positions.

To ensure you won't aim too low, be patient during your job search and don't sell yourself short. Believe in yourself and believe that you can find a job that will be a great fit. The right job is out there for you; it just takes time and effort to find it.

Form a support group

It can be difficult (and sometimes discouraging) to find a job if you are going through the job search process alone. Try forming a support group of family and close friends to provide encouragement and assistance while you're on your job seeking journey. For example, enlist your sister, your best friend, or your significant other to review and provide feedback on your resume, LinkedIn profile, and cover letters.

Ask your parents (or a few close friends) to role-play with you by conducting mock interviews. Have your dad act as the hiring manager while your mom listens and takes notes. Then switch, and have your mom role-play the hiring manager while your father watches and takes notes. Discuss what both observed and consider things you can do to improve your interview presence. Getting family and friends involved in your job search process can be a great way to infuse energy and enthusiasm into the work you'll need to complete.

Weed out the "negative Nellies"

While you are building a network of supportive people, don't forget to weed out the people I call "negative Nellies." These can be friends, family members, or acquaintances who always seem to make negative comments about anything you're doing while looking for a job. One way you can identify these people is by the way you feel when you're around them. Often times, you'll feel like all the energy has been drained from your body. That is because it probably has – these people are human energy vampires who will suck your energy dry with their negativity.

When you identify a situation where this is happening with a specific person, it is time to re-evaluate your relationship with them. Is the relationship mutually beneficial? If not, don't be afraid to have a discussion with this person to tell them you don't appreciate their constant negativity. Let them know you are surrounding yourself with only people who are positive and will help bring out the best in you, and that given their current behavior, you may need to end the friendship if they cannot change.

One of the best things you can do for yourself during your job search process (and for the rest of your life) is to carefully choose the people with whom you surround yourself. If you want to achieve your life's purpose, then be selective about the people with whom you associate. *Choose people who will lift you up and help you fly, not those who will hold you back from achieving your dreams.*

Don't forget to exude passion and energy

Sometimes it is not a lack of prep work that keeps you from obtaining your dream job – it might just be that you're not exuding passion or energy for the position. Leah was discouraged with her job search and hired me to help her. *"I'm really good at what I do, but I'm not a dynamic interviewee,"* Leah told me during our first meeting. *"My resume gets me the telephone interview. That gets me the in-person interview. But then I never get the job offer."*

She took a sip of coffee and sighed as she set her cup on the table. *"It's happened over and over. I practice. I study. I do everything right. But then I don't get the job. What's wrong with me?"*

Sometimes, like Leah, a candidate can do everything right when it comes to preparing for an interview. And after reviewing what Leah had been doing as prep work, she had done a great job. But for many hiring managers, like myself, there are often other attributes we look for in candidates during job interviews that might not be specifically called out in the job posting. A friend of mine sums up these general attributes quite well. He says he looks for "attitude, aptitude, and promotability."

In other words, he looks for someone who has a positive attitude and is energetic, who is intelligent and has the ability to learn new things, and who has long-term potential with the company and could be promoted up the ranks.

In addition to these attributes, I look for candidates with accountability and the ability to implement. By this, I mean individuals who hold themselves accountable – for completing and implementing projects, continuing their personal development, taking proactive steps to improve their skills each year, and accountable for their mistakes and learning from them. I also look for people who can implement projects and ideas and who have achieved demonstrable results in previous positions.

While a hiring manager can see some of these attributes by reading the job candidate's resume, most are attributes that come across while interviewing someone in person. So Leah and I conducted some practice interviews. *Her problem?* Even though she was highly professional and had good qualifications, she seemed very "flat" during her interview. With each passing minute, Leah's energy level decreased and her voice became more monotone.

Leah just wasn't selling me on her passion and drive to obtain the job. She also wasn't conveying the appropriate work examples to show her determination to take on more challenging work and learn new skills. So we took a break from our mock interview and I explained to Leah those "other attributes" I generally look for in job candidates:

- Attitude
- Aptitude
- Promotability
- Accountability
- Ability to implement

Leah caught on quickly and began telling me about examples of the results she had achieved leading various projects. She also explained how she had proactively contributed to improving processes in several previous jobs and then described what she had done over the last year as part of her personal development plan.

And guess what? As she was telling me all this, Leah became more and more excited, and her passion for her work was clearly visible. That was exactly the energetic attitude she needed to get across to hiring managers during job interviews.

What Leah, Patricia, and Melanie learned is that a positive attitude and inner confidence play an important role in the job search process. If you believe in yourself and believe in your abilities, this will come across in your attitude. It will also shine through during your job interviews.

**CHAPTER 32
KEY TAKEAWAYS**

Finding a job that is a good fit requires a thoughtful, strategic approach. The job search process isn't a sprint; it is more like running a marathon. No matter how painful it feels, you must remain emotionally strong throughout and give yourself inner pep talks as motivation. Weed out the "negative Nellies" and focus on building a network of supportive people.

NEGOTIATE YOUR JOB OFFER

I touched on this topic briefly in Chapter 20 when we discussed how to answer the "salary question." I'm going into full detail in this chapter, because it's incredibly important, and as a career coach, I've learned a sad truth: Women rarely negotiate their salaries. Most of the women I've coached tell me they have never even considered negotiating their salary for a new job because the idea of it made them uncomfortable. However, being a good negotiator is a critical success factor for climbing the career ladder and doing well in business. Some people seem to have a knack for negotiating, but anyone can learn the skill with a little research and practice.

Negotiating a job offer isn't as difficult as you might think. I've watched women go from being scared of negotiating to loving it. How? They changed their approach and started thinking about negotiating as a simple process and a thoughtful interaction with others. When it comes to negotiating a starting salary, here are my recommendations:

Fully understand the job. Make sure you understand all of the responsibilities and expectations for the position.

Educate yourself on the company. Ensure you've asked and understood how the company reviews employee performance as well as the process for pay raises and promotions.

Arm yourself with salary information. Spend adequate time researching salary ranges for similar jobs in your area, industry, and geography. There are many websites that provide salary information, including: salary. com, payscale.com, indeed.com, careeronestop.org, glassdoor.com, and jobsearchintelligence.com.

Know your strengths and differentiators. What makes you special and unique from everyone else? Use the exercise in Chapter 7 (Conduct a Personal

S.W.O.T. Analysis) to understand your differentiators and the special skills or experiences that could make you a more valuable employee. Write these differentiators down – you can leverage them to negotiate an increased starting salary with the hiring manager.

Determine how much you'd like to make. Consider what you've made in your last few jobs, the results of your online salary research, and your strengths and differentiators. Given that information, determine your target salary.

Decide on an appropriate salary range. Based on your research of similar jobs in your geography and industry, come up with what you think would be an appropriate salary range for the job. Your target salary should fall within this salary range.

Define your "walk-away" point. Now that you've determined your target salary and an appropriate salary range, think about the minimum salary you're willing to accept and why you'd accept that amount. Then, consider the reasons why you would be unwilling to accept a lower amount. Write these reasons down, as you may need to discuss them with the hiring manager during the salary negotiation.

Practice your negotiation skills. Ask a friend or family member to play the role of a hiring manager who has offered you a salary that is lower than what you want. Then practice what you will say and how you will say it to persuade the hiring manager to increase the offer.

It is in the hiring manager's best interest to carefully determine the salary offers to new employees. They need to make sure their compensation offers are internally and externally competitive and that they don't offer a too-high or too-low salary, given the education, experience levels, and productivity of the employees currently working in the same or similar positions. At most companies, a lot of research and analysis goes into every compensation offer before a job offer is ever made.

That isn't to say you can't or shouldn't negotiate for a higher salary – by all means, go for it if you believe you have good reasons for the request. This is especially true if you have specialized skills or training that are in short supply or worth more to the company. Most hiring managers don't automatically try to low-ball salary offers, but they will usually start with an amount that is slightly lower than what they are willing to pay, because they assume the candidate will negotiate upward.

Jamie had received a verbal job offer with a starting salary just below her target. She was excited, but called me with a question. *"I'd be willing to accept the slightly lower offer if the company would pay for me to go back to school to earn my MBA. Is that something I could negotiate with the hiring manager?"*

Considering other potential benefits to negotiate (instead of trying to obtain a higher salary) is also an option. Benefits are an adjunct to an employee's base pay and can include discretionary benefits and legally required benefits:

Discretionary benefits. These are not required by law; they are provided at the discretion of the company and are generally employer paid. Examples include: life insurance, paid time off, holiday pay, vacation pay, tuition reimbursement or assistance programs, wellness programs and childcare programs or assistance.

Legally required benefits. These were established by the U.S. government to protect employees from catastrophic events and include unemployment benefits and disability benefits.

Discretionary benefits have evolved over the years and become methods for attracting and retaining highly qualified candidates. Creative benefits, when tailored to match the needs and values of the employees, can help companies become more market-competitive, sometimes without adding a lot of costs. Examples include: a casual dress policy, dry-cleaning services, athletic facilities, on-site day care, a health clinic for medical needs, even flexible work schedules. While these types of benefits do increase job satisfaction and employee productivity, they are typically not negotiable.

What can you negotiate as part of your starting salary? The use of perquisites or "perks." These can include sign-on bonuses, additional vacation days, use of a company vehicle, relocation expenses, annual medical exams, or flying in business or first class instead of coach. However, these types of "perks" are usually only for jobs at the executive level or for positions of critical importance where it is difficult to find qualified talent.

When the economic recession occurred, many companies were forced to reduce expenses and cut the amount and types of discretionary benefits previously available. Because of this, it has become difficult for candidates to use benefits or perks as part of salary negotiation. There is often also a high volume of qualified candidates who are willing to accept jobs at lower salaries with fewer benefits – making companies less willing to offer perks.

For example, a sales manager shared this recent hiring situation with me. When he gave the verbal job offer to the candidate he'd chosen for an open sales position, the job seeker requested two additional items: a $20,000 sign-on bonus and a guaranteed payout to his first year of variable commissions. The hiring manager and the vice president of sales both chuckled in private and joked, *"Who does this guy think he is, a professional baseball player?"* The point being that employers have so many qualified candidates to choose from right now that almost no employer needs to include additional benefits to attract candidates (or agree to any candidate requests).

I *am* seeing negotiable benefits being used in certain positions, such as within research and development or at the senior executive level, where highly specialized education and/or experience is necessary. The computer-programming field uses negotiable benefits as well, due to the high demand and low supply of programmers.

While you can choose to inquire as to what other benefits (discretionary and negotiable) are available, don't automatically assume an employer will be willing to negotiate beyond the stated salary and compensation package.

Jamie followed the process outlined in this chapter and had a discussion with the hiring manager about the starting salary. While she wasn't able to get the employer to agree to pay for her MBA, she was able to negotiate a slightly higher salary and tuition assistance (up to a certain amount per year) to go back to school. Because she took the time to negotiate what she wanted, Jamie felt much better when she accepted the adjusted job offer. So remember, negotiation is a skill you can hone. But, it is up to *you* to get what you want and what you deserve.

The secret to salary negotiation

If you want to make the salary negotiation process easier, during the initial telephone discussion with the HR representative, ask him or her for the budgeted salary range. Explain that you want to make sure your salary expectations are appropriate, given the job and responsibilities. That way, you'll have the salary range information prior to your telephone or in-person interview with the hiring manager. And, if the pay is way beneath your expectations, you won't waste your time or the hiring manager's time.

CHAPTER 33
KEY TAKEAWAYS

Be prepared to negotiate your starting salary and learn to consider the first offer a starting point for discussion. Understand the going rates in your geography and industry for the position you seek, define your target salary and an appropriate pay range, and determine your "walk away" amount. Have talking points ready for why you believe you deserve a higher amount.

CHOOSE BETWEEN TWO JOB OPPORTUNITIES

A former client Catherine approached me with an unusual career situation during the economic recession. *Her problem?* She was stressed out and didn't know what to do because she had two job offers, but couldn't decide which to take. Neither was her dream job, but both paid more than she currently made, and one could lead to a human resources manager position – her career goal.

Most job opportunities are not quite the dream job we want. In Catherine's case, trying to make a choice had become overly stressful and was causing decision paralysis. I suggested Catherine use this process of analysis to help her fully explore her options:

Brainstorm. Write down everything that matters most when it comes to your job or career. This list might include promotion opportunities, salary, commission structure, company culture, type of work, control over the projects on which you will work, bonus eligibility, benefits such as medical coverage, hours of work per week, or the amount of business travel.

Prioritize. After brainstorming, read through the list and prioritize the items from most important to least.

Analyze. Make two columns next to your prioritized list, one for each job opportunity. Think through each item and how well each job will provide for/satisfy each priority, writing notes in both columns.

Review. Go over your notes and ask yourself if one opportunity meets more of your priorities than the other? If so, why?

This isn't always an easy process. Choosing one job over another often requires trade-offs. In Catherine's situation, one job had nothing to do with human resources, but was much closer to her home and paid more. The other job was in line with her career goal and could lead to future promotion opportunities, but it had a longer commute, a lower salary, and fewer medical benefits.

While this won't completely alleviate the risk of moving into a new job, it does help you make the most informed decision possible.

While working through this exercise, it eventually becomes clear which job opportunity is the better fit given your career goals, needs, and wants. While this won't completely alleviate the risk of moving into a new job, it does help you to make the most informed decision possible.

Catherine decided to take the job that would get her closer to her career goal of becoming an HR manager. Even though she would need to drive a little farther to work and initially wouldn't make as much money, these were sacrifices she was willing to make for the chance to work in HR. As Catherine discovered, sometimes, short-term sacrifices are worth the long-term career payoff.

Another client, Kristin, went through this analysis process, but at the end, she still couldn't choose between her two job opportunities. *Kristin's problem?* She had analysis paralysis. She kept on conducting more and more analysis to compare the two jobs, but just couldn't make a decision.

That is when I suggested we toss a coin. I pulled one out and asked Kristin to choose one job as "heads" and the other job as "tails." She looked at me like I was crazy, but I tossed the coin and let it fall to the ground. Kristin rushed over to it and looked disappointed when she examined the coin. *"Oh, I guess I was hoping it would land on the other side,"* she said, and then handed me the coin.

"Then the other job is the opportunity you actually want," I told her. I had to laugh because she looked at me again like I was crazy. *"It might not be a very conventional way to make this decision, but it can be a helpful way to uncover your true feelings between two opportunities,"* I explained.

"If you find yourself hoping for one of the two options or if you're not happy with the outcome, then you've just discovered the job you really want," I added. *"When the coin landed and you saw that it was heads, you were disappointed because you hoped it would land tails up. That means, in your heart, you're actually more excited about the other job opportunity."*

Kristin shook her head in disbelief. *"I just can't believe it worked. As soon as you flipped the coin in the air I was hoping it would land tails up. I guess, deep down, I really did know which of the two jobs I wanted."*

Sometimes we tend to make things more complicated than they should be. Flipping a coin is simple, and it removes the brain from the equation and lets the heart show which opportunity is of most interest.

Shannon had a similar situation. She was presented with two job opportunities after having been let go during the recession due to downsizing. *Shannon's problem?* One job opportunity would give her internal satisfaction, but she wouldn't make enough money to support her family. The other job provided a much higher salary, a bonus opportunity, and would allow her family to be economically stable, but the work would not provide the same level of satisfaction.

As we explored Shannon's options, she realized that taking the more satisfying job would require her to find part-time work in addition to a full-time job, which meant more time away from her children. So we discussed how Shannon could seek satisfaction in other ways, such as volunteering for interesting job assignments in the higher paying position or taking up a hobby outside of work that would help her achieve personal life goals.

In the end, Shannon chose the higher paying job that offered less fulfilling work and then she found ways outside of the office to make her life more meaningful. She was also hopeful that she could prove herself in the position and, in the future, move on to a more challenging job with her new employer. Sometimes, satisfying economic needs must come before personal ambitions, but there are always creative ways to find gratification.

**CHAPTER 34
KEY TAKEAWAYS**

Having to choose between two or more job opportunities isn't a bad thing. When this situation occurs, try a process of analysis to fully explore your options, or, opt for a more unconventional method, such as flipping a coin. The coin toss can be a helpful way to uncover your true feelings between two opportunities.

CHAPTER 35

NEVER ACCEPT A COUNTER OFFER WHEN YOU RESIGN

It was a moment in my career that I will never forget. I had accepted a new job at a different company and when I went into my boss's office to quit, with resignation letter in hand, he offered me a higher salary if I would remain in my current job.

Even if you think this would never happen to you, it is best to prepare in advance so you'll feel comfortable with your response, which should always be: *"No, thank you."* Surprised that I'm telling you to decline your manager's counter offer? Here's why…

If you followed the process I outlined in Chapter 2 – to analyze the reasons why you want to change jobs – then you'd already have identified the issues that were within your manager's or your ability to control. And you'd already have worked through ways of fixing those issues. If you felt you were underpaid, you'd have asked your boss for a raise. If you were bored in your job and wanted more challenging work, you would have discussed this with your manager and asked him or her to assign you to projects or tasks that will broaden and deepen your work experience. If a lengthy commute was lowering the quality of your life, you'd have negotiated to work from home a few days a week.

Whatever the reasons were for wanting to change jobs, you would have analyzed them and made every attempt to fix the issues that were possible to fix. So what does that leave you? *Issues that weren't fixable – the deal-breakers.* They were the reasons you went out and found a new job that better fits your career requirements or goals. So why would you suddenly want to stay in your job just because your boss offered you more money?

If you lacked career growth opportunities, would that go away just because you've been offered a higher salary? Probably not. Let's say one of your reasons for leaving was so you could work for a small, start-up company and learn how to become a successful entrepreneur. If you currently work for a large bureaucratic corporation, would making more money (or other perks) change your work environment? No.

If your boss is insecure and his or her behavior has demonstrated an unwillingness to be supportive of your career development, would that behavior change with your counter offer? Highly unlikely. In fact, if you accept your manager's counter offer, his or her behavior toward you will likely get worse over time because you'll be labeled a 'problem' employee.

If you previously couldn't get a raise from your boss when you provided proof that you're underpaid, ask yourself: *"Why is my manager offering me a raise now that I'm resigning?"* If you weren't valuable enough to be given a raise before, why would your boss be willing to give you more money now? Most likely, it is not because you've suddenly become a more valuable employee. It's because your manager doesn't want to deal with the work disruption your departure could create. Let me state that one more time to be sure you understand… *your manager doesn't suddenly think you've become a more valuable employee. He or she doesn't want to deal with the disruption your departure could create.*

Don't let your ego or feeling flattered that you're being offered more money cloud your judgment or cause you to make a bad decision.

Don't waiver on your decision to change jobs. You took the time to identify your reasons for leaving. You worked to fix all the issues that were within your control. There were issues that weren't fixable and these were your deal-breakers. Because you couldn't change the deal-breakers, you found a new job that was a better match to your career goals and aspirations. Don't let your ego or feeling flattered that you're being offered more money cloud your judgment or cause you to make a bad decision. You already did your homework, so feel secure about the process you went through to seek a different job.

If you begin to second-guess your acceptance of the new job and consider accepting your manager's counter offer, think about what else would change if you stayed (besides receiving more money). Review each of your reasons for wanting to switch jobs and take an honest look at your deal-breaker issues. Will they somehow magically disappear if you accepted the counter offer? Nope. So look your boss in the eyes, smile nicely, and say *"No, thank you"* to that counter offer.

CHAPTER 35
KEY TAKEAWAYS

You identified your reasons for leaving your current job. You tried to fix all the issues that were within your control, but there were deal-breakers that weren't fixable, so you found a job that is a better match to your career goals. When you resign, don't waiver on your decision to change jobs if your boss offers you more money to stay. You already did your homework, so feel secure about the process you went through to seek a different job.

GRACEFULLY QUIT YOUR CURRENT JOB

You just accepted a new job. Congratulations! Way to go! You feel great. You're so excited, you feel as if you could fly. Then it hits you. Now you have to quit your job. Ugh.

Don't worry, just follow these steps to exit your current job in a manner that is professional and will leave your good reputation intact:

Step 1: Make sure you've finalized the details with your new employer. Don't quit your current job until everything about your new job is negotiated and ready to go. Salary and compensation plan? Check. Benefits package? Check. Company policies reviewed? Check. Start date? Check. On-boarding process ready? Check. Signed offer letter or employment contract? Check. You get the idea.

Step 2: Plan how you'll transfer your responsibilities. Don't leave your boss inundated with unfinished work. Determine a transition plan for your responsibilities and any unfinished projects. Create a list with your recommendations on how your work can be shifted to others in the department until your position can be filled. Your mission is to make your departure go as smoothly as possible for your manager.

Step 3: Write your resignation letter. I like to think of a resignation letter more like a brief thank you note. Your resignation letter should explain your gratitude for having had the opportunity to work at XYZ company and with your boss, and include the date of your last day on the job. Keep it simple, because your resignation letter will most likely go into your personnel file – where it will remain indefinitely.

Step 4: Determine your "story." Think through how you will explain your departure to your manager and coworkers. Whatever reasons you provide, keep your story consistent and keep your reasons positive, not negative. For example, DON'T say, *"I'm leaving because you're a jerk. No matter how many times I asked, you refused to give me opportunities to lead projects."* Instead, say, *"I'm excited about my new job because it will give me the opportunity to strengthen my skills in people management and project management by leading cross-functional and cross-cultural projects."*

Step 5: Tell your manager before anyone else. Your manager deserves to be told first, so refrain from saying anything to coworkers until you've met with your boss. Also, consider how you'll handle the situation if your boss makes you a counteroffer to stay in your job, as we discussed in the last chapter.

Step 6: Quit in person, and bring your resignation letter with you. Quitting a job is like breaking up in a relationship. It is always best and most respectful if you do it in person and can provide closure. If your boss works in a different geographic location, let's say you're in Seattle and your boss is in Boston, then try to meet with him or her in person when either you're in Boston or they're in Seattle. If the timing just doesn't work, make an appointment to speak with them over the telephone. You can then follow up with a brief email and attach your resignation letter.

Step 7: Give adequate notice. Providing a two-week notice is a global norm. However, if your job is complex and will be difficult to fill or if you are in a higher-level management position, be prepared to provide additional time for your employer to find your replacement. Offer to train your replacement if your position can be filled before your last day.

Step 8: Reach agreement with your boss on how others will be told. During your resignation meeting with your manager, ask him or her how they would like others in the company to be told. My recommendation as a career coach is that you should tell coworkers individually and you should volunteer to write a short email your boss can then distribute within the department. If you are in a higher-level management position, your boss will most likely need to send an email announcement company-wide or at least within a specific geography. Discuss this with him or her and offer to write the draft version of the email notification.

Step 9: Meet individually with mentors and sponsors within the company. Beyond your own department, if you have mentors or anyone within the company who has acted as your sponsor, quickly schedule time to meet with each person. Let them know you're leaving and why. In most cases, this shouldn't be surprising news because they will be well aware of what is going on in your career. Be sure to thank them for all their help, let them know that you plan to keep in touch, and then regularly provide them with your career updates so you won't lose them from your support team.

Step 10: Remain professional throughout the process. No matter how you feel, avoid quitting in anger or using any unsavory methods to quit. Treating others with compassion and respect will always get you farther in life. Besides, some time in the future, you may want to work for this employer again. The business world is incredibly interlinked; don't do anything that might burn a bridge. And who knows? Your current manager might someday switch companies and become your boss again or a previous employer might acquire the company where you've just accepted your new job. Be on your best behavior so you will leave the company on a positive note, leaving the door open for future employment and ensuring a good job reference.

Step 11: Remove personal items from your work area. If you begin cleaning out your office before telling people you are leaving, you will set off a gossip firestorm. So, wait until *after* you've notified your boss and coworkers to clean out your workspace. Take personal items home and ensure you leave your office looking neat and clean for the next person.

Step 12: Be prepared for the exit interview. Speaking as a former hiring manager and employer, don't be afraid if you're asked into an exit interview. It is usually HR personnel who conduct the exit interviews with the purpose of uncovering areas where the company can improve or identifying when there may be issues with a specific manager (such as when employee turnover is high in a certain department).

Go into the exit interview ready to tell the "story" of why you're leaving and avoid gossiping, whining, or trashing your boss or the company. Instead, be ready to explain a few reasons why you enjoyed working at the company. Also, be prepared to offer one or two honest suggestions for improvement, such as *"In thinking about my employment here, I wish there had been a formal training program when I started my job, so I could have gotten up to speed faster."*

Or, *"It would have been helpful to have had educational or training opportunities to learn more about project management and cultural training on ways to work with people from other countries."*

Step 13: Be prepared to be escorted out by security. If your new employer happens to be a direct competitor of the company where you currently work, you may be asked to leave immediately upon your resignation. Also, don't be surprised if security personnel are assigned to watch you while you clean out your workspace and then escort you to your vehicle – this is to ensure you take only personal belongings and no company confidential information to the competitor. Don't be offended if this happens, it is typical protocol when someone quits and goes to work for a direct competitor.

A few additional tips to help you quit your current job respectfully:

Work as hard as you can, all the way up until the final minute on your last day. The best way to ensure you leave on a positive note is to work hard at your job and at ensuring a smooth transition right up until the time you're walking out the door on your last day and waving goodbye to coworkers. Slacking off on your work after you've resigned will only damage your reputation and ruin the chances of using your manager or the employer as a positive reference.

Don't speak negatively about past employers or bosses. During the resignation process and after you've left the company, avoid saying anything negative about the employer, your manager, or your coworkers. The old saying holds true, "If you can't say anything nice, don't say anything at all." Holding your tongue will also ensure you won't damage your own reputation.

Don't do anything illegal. Even if you hate your boss and can't stand your employer, be a professional and leave gracefully. Don't do anything that could jeopardize your career, such as sabotaging the company's database or stealing confidential company documents or information. Leave with the highest level of integrity.

Keep in touch. If you left positively and with your reputation intact, don't lose track of your network. Keep in touch with everyone of importance at your previous employer. You never know when you might want to be rehired by a former employer or when you'll need a reference or a recommendation from a former boss, colleague, or direct report.

Update social media profiles. Once you've started your new job, don't forget to update your social media profiles, such as LinkedIn. And while you're at it, update your resume too.

CHAPTER 36
KEY TAKEAWAYS

When it comes time to quit your current job, follow the steps outlined in this chapter so you can exit in a graceful and professional manner that will leave your good reputation intact.

EPILOGUE

As you work through the steps in this book, remember that finding a job isn't a sprint to the finish line. The job seeking process is more like running in a marathon – you must be emotionally strong throughout, it can sometimes be painful, and you must be willing to give yourself inner pep talks as motivation.

Consider your job search a journey of self-discovery, one that will help you learn more about yourself, your unique qualities, and areas you could work to improve. Be willing to give yourself a personal "time out" to discover the career you truly want and to define your career goals and aspirations. Use your research and investigative abilities to seek out the jobs you find most interesting and exciting and that are a good match to your skills, experience, and education.

While you are on your job search journey, be fully present and consciously "awake." By this, I mean, don't sleepwalk through the process, merely checking off steps as you complete them – take the time to think about what you're doing and what you're learning. Embrace every day with awareness, compassion, and intelligent choice. Each day, ask yourself: *"What have I learned?"* Maybe you found out something new about yourself, about a potential employer, or even about a potential boss. Maybe you discovered a certain job would be a great fit for you (or a terrible fit). Think about what you're learning, and file that information in your memory for future use.

Take each day one day at a time, enjoying the process and practicing gratitude throughout your entire job search. Begin a journal and, every night, write down at least one thing for which you're grateful or thankful. Life truly is a gift, and the job search process should be savored as if every day you are being given a precious gift to open. How will you use the special gifts you receive? How will you use what you are learning to achieve your life's purpose?

As you follow the guidance in this book and create your plan to get you from where you are now to where you want to be, take ownership of your situation and the choices you make – then watch as events unfold in your life. Owning your situation and accepting the events that occur will allow you to focus on changing the things that are within your power to change. To be successful, you must actively participate in your career – don't sit on the sidelines! *Treat your career like a business and treat yourself like a product that you continuously improve, year after year.*

Just remember, while a fancy looking resume, a voluminous portfolio of work, or an incredibly chic interview outfit might get you noticed, it won't get you hired. What *will* get you the job is what is in your head and in your heart – it is about your knowledge and your passion for the job and for life.

I wish you all the best on your job search journey. You can do it!

~ Your Career Coach, Lisa

RESOURCES

Now that you've finished reading the book and are ready to take action, here are additional resources to help you accomplish your goals and reach your career aspirations. They address the most commonly asked questions I receive, including why you should create and update your own resume, how to get rehired by a former employer, tips on applying for a job internally, tips for career changers, and how asking for constructive criticism can change your career. You can find even more tips and resources online at www.career-womaninc.com. Your success starts with you! *And a little guidance from me.*

WHY YOU SHOULD CREATE AND UPDATE YOUR OWN RESUME

"But I just want you to re-write my resume. Can't you just re-write my resume for me?" she pleaded.

Thus ended my conversation with a woman who had called to inquire about hiring me as a career coach. She didn't like the answer I gave her, which was, *"No."*

Sometimes in our careers, as in life, taking on challenging tasks can lead to personal growth and learning. This potential client didn't see it that way — she wanted me to do everything for her. Here is the conversation (condensed) that led us down that discussion path...

Jane: *"I want to hire you as my career coach."*

Me: *"Let's first talk about the type of career help you're seeking."*

Jane: *"I just need you to re-write my resume. I don't like my job so I want to find another position in a different industry. I haven't updated it since I got this job about 10 years ago."*

Me: *"Tell me why your job is making you unhappy, and, what type of job would you like to have?"*

Jane: *"What do you mean?"*

Me: *"What jobs have you looked at and what are the areas in the job descriptions that interest you?"*

Jane: *"I haven't been researching any jobs. And why should I look at job descriptions? I just want to update my resume."*

Me: *"Generally, the best way to update a resume is to customize it to the position to which you're applying. Doing this requires analyzing the job description and requirements and then tailoring your resume to showcase your skills and accomplishments most relevant to the job."*

Jane: *"Can't you just figure that out for me? I don't have time to think about that stuff myself. My life is one tornado after another and I don't have any time for myself as it is."*

Me: *"Sounds like you must work a lot of hours or have quite a few family activities going on."*

Jane: *"Um, not really. I'm only allowed to work 40 hours a week because they hate paying us overtime. And I'm single and none of my family lives in the area."*

(Jumping to the end of our discussion...)

Me: *"Let me see if I understand what you're saying. You no longer enjoy your current job or industry. You don't know what you'd like to do next, and, you don't want to explore this yourself. You don't have the time or interest in looking at positions posted online to determine which jobs interest you. You want to hire someone to re-write your resume without actually having to be involved in the process yourself."*

Jane: *"Exactly! Now you understand."*

Me: *"Unfortunately, that is not how I conduct my career coaching practice. I cannot re-write your resume without your participation. Updating your resume means we spend time analyzing your skills, experience, education, and accomplishments. It requires uncovering your strengths and weaknesses as well as looking at potential industries, companies, and jobs of interest to you. It includes analyzing the job descriptions you'd like to apply to and targeting your resume to the requirements of those positions. I can guide you and assist you throughout this process, but it requires your active participation."*

Our discussion ended after I turned Jane down as a client. No matter what I said, she could not understand why she needed to participate for the process to be effective, and she wasn't the first person I've encountered with this attitude.

If you are considering hiring someone to merely re-write your resume – I offer the following thoughts:

- Creating or re-writing your resume can be a challenge, but life is all about challenges and about learning from them. It is through challenges that we grow the most.
- You may believe you have little to no time in your life for career activities such as updating your resume, but consider the karmic idea that forcing yourself to carve out "me time" is how you'll be able to overcome any swirling chaos around you.
- Before you attempt to create or write your resume, take the time to define your career aspirations and to look at industries, companies, and jobs of interest. Also, consider your strengths and weaknesses and analyze how well you match up against the job requirements.

Your career requires your active participation and you need to be the captain of your own ship. Don't hand off your career development responsibilities and tasks to someone else. Seek others for career *guidance,* not for ownership.

HOW TO GET REHIRED BY A FORMER EMPLOYER

As the unemployment rate continues to decrease, many people who had lost their jobs because of corporate downsizing are returning to their former employers for job opportunities. While it may not be possible to get your old job back, if you enjoyed working at a certain company (and left on a positive note), then getting rehired is definitely an option. But before you apply for any positions, here are eight tips to consider:

Tip #1: Find job opportunities of interest. On your previous employer's website, search for open positions that are of interest and download those job descriptions. Carefully read each one, highlighting key requirements.

Tip #2: Update and customize your resume. Tailor your resume to those positions in a way that showcases your skills, education, and accomplishments that are most relevant to the job requirements.

Tip #3: Define your network. Make a list of everyone you worked with or knew at your previous company so you can see your network. LinkedIn is a helpful tool to accomplish this task.

Tip #4: Re-establish relationships. Using whatever means you're comfortable with (LinkedIn, telephone, email, in-person, etc.), connect with key people to re-establish relationships. Focus on making contact with coworkers who saw your work firsthand and could be your "inside coach" to help you get back into the company. Also, find out what has happened or changed since you left.

Tip #5: Spread the word. Let your network know you're interested in getting re-hired. Offer to email them your updated resume and ask them to submit it to hiring managers for positions of interest. Need references? This is also a good time to ask key people within your network to be included on your list of references or ask them for a recommendation (either a formal letter or a recommendation via LinkedIn).

Tip #6: Connect with HR. Did you work with or know anyone in human resources at your previous employer, specifically in the area of recruiting? Contact them to let them know you are interested in open positions that fit your background.

Tip #7: Stay current. Regularly review the company's website for current job postings, and contact hiring managers for positions of interest.

Tip #8: Prepare answers. If you weren't part of corporate downsizing due to the recession, have an answer ready for why you left and where you worked after leaving. Be able to explain why you want to come back and the value you would bring to the company if you were rehired.

TIPS ON APPLYING FOR A
JOB WITHIN YOUR COMPANY

Are you looking for a new job within your current company? Don't assume just because you already work there, that you'll have an advantage in obtaining the job. In fact, most hiring managers are even tougher on internal candidates than external ones. That's because they know internal candidates have access to more company personnel and a lot more information about the position than an external candidate. So if you don't do your homework, be prepared for poor results.

Sally is an example of what can go wrong when you skip the important preparation steps I've explained in this book. Sally was an internal candidate who had applied for one of the open positions within the marketing team I managed. Since she already worked at the company and had access to the employees in my department, my assumption was that she would be well prepared for her job interview. I was wrong.

When I asked her questions about our newly released product, she was unable to answer. When I asked how she thought the product introduction from our number one competitor would impact sales of our newly released product, she didn't have an opinion. When I asked her what she thought it would take to be successful in the position, she pulled out the job posting and pointed to the list of job requirements. The interview spiraled downward at a rapid pace due to her lack of preparation.

Several weeks after the interview, Sally asked me to have coffee. As we sat and talked, she apologized for the interview. She explained that for many years, new roles had sort of fallen into her lap without any effort on her part. Sally told me she hadn't taken the interview process seriously enough and she had wrongly assumed that since I'd seen her at various meetings and knew who she was, that I would automatically hire her, due to her success in her current job.

But here's the thing, I wasn't her manager so I didn't know anything more about her than what I'd read on her resume. Yes, I'd seen her around the office and during various meetings, and she had usually been well prepared for discussions. That's what made her lack of preparation for the job interview all the more perplexing. During the interview, she hadn't been able to convince me why I should hire her for the position or that she understood what it would take to be successful as a marketing manager.

After the job interview, I could tell that Sally was embarrassed to see me during meetings and sensed an awkward tension when we would pass each other in the hallways, so I was glad when we had the opportunity to sit down for a chat. It was a tough lesson for her to learn, but the good news is that she did learn from her mistake.

About a year later she told me that she had taken our discussion to heart and used what she'd learned to prepare for an interview in another division of the company. She obtained the job because she was a good fit and because she had spent time preparing: she learned everything she could about the position and the department, spoke with several employees currently in the same roles, researched the skills and experience necessary to be successful in the position, and prepared answers to potential interview questions.

What I hope you'll learn from this story is that it takes just as much work to obtain a new job at your current place of work – and sometimes more – because the expectation is that you'll be more prepared than an external candidate. So don't take anything for granted, and follow these tips to help you be successful.

DO:

- Take the interview process seriously and prepare for your internal job interview by following the steps explained in this book. Especially important are customizing your resume to the job, writing a customized cover letter, creating a portfolio of work examples, preparing for the interview, and obtaining internal references/sponsors who will vouch for your background, skills, and work performance.

- Speak to employees who are already in the job you want and find out: what they think about the job, the good aspects and the challenges faced in the position, what they believe it takes to be successful in the job, any advice they may have for you for the interview process.
- Meet with the HR representative (often called an "HR business partner") responsible for the department you want to work in. Let the person know which position you want, and discuss the job's responsibilities and requirements, your background (knowledge, experience, skills, and education), and your "fit" for the position. Tell the HR person that you'd like to apply for the position and ask for their feedback and thoughts on whether they believe you could be a successful candidate.
- Let your manager know if you decide to apply for the open position. Many companies require that the current manager be notified whenever an employee applies for another position within the company. Even if this rule doesn't exit, it's always best to be honest with your boss and let him or her know that you're applying for another job and the reasons why. For example, your reasons might be to gain additional or different work experience, take on higher level or more challenging work, move into a position where you manage others, etc.
- Gain the support of your manager. The best possible sponsor/ reference you could have is your boss, so solicit their support to obtain the job you want. And don't forget to let him or her know how much you've appreciated working for them.
- Make a list of employees familiar with your work performance and who also know the hiring manager. Let each person know about the internal position for which you're applying, and find out if they would be willing to help you obtain the job. These are people who could put in a good word about you to the hiring manager or even act as internal references or sponsors during the interview process.
- Follow the normal job application process and submit all required documents in the format requested (usually online).

- Take a hard copy of your resume to the hiring manager and introduce yourself in person after you've submitted it online. Let them know you've just applied online for the open position (state the job title) and that you also wanted to drop off your resume in person so they would be able to put a face with the name on the resume. Then hand the hiring manager your resume and let them know you're looking forward to speaking with them during the interview process.
- Write a customized thank you note to the hiring manager after your interview. If you get the job, be sure to thank everyone who helped, especially your current boss.

DON'T:
- Assume you'll be given the job just because you already work at the company. You must *earn* the right to be given a job offer.
- Assume the hiring manager knows about you, your background, your education, or the quality/quantity of your work performance. Be prepared to explain why you're the best person for the job and demonstrate the high quality of your work.
- Drop the productivity level in your current job while you're going through the interview process for another position. Managers speak to each other and negative work performance could hurt your chances of obtaining the job. Keep focused and stay on track with tasks and projects.
- Forget to look the part during the interview. Even if you work in a casual office environment, take it a step up when it comes to your interview attire, so you'll really shine.
- Get upset or angry if you didn't get the job. The good news is that you've gotten to know another hiring manager in the company. Build on that relationship to positively position yourself when another job becomes available.

If you didn't get the job, the best thing you can do is move on gracefully and use it as a learning experience. Ask the HR representative and the hiring manager if they are willing to provide feedback. Let them know that you'd like to understand, from their perspective, things you did well and areas (skills/ experience) you could work on as part of your career development. How you handle yourself when you don't get a job can often affect whether you obtain the next job working for that hiring manager, so always act professionally. Use every interview experience (even if it was bad) as a learning opportunity so you'll be better prepared the next time you apply for a job.

TIPS FOR CAREER CHANGERS

One of the questions I'm often asked by job seekers who want to switch careers is, *"How do I figure out if my skills are transferable?"* Here are four tips to determine this: 1) Analyze the job requirements, 2) Analyze yourself against the job requirements, 3) Seek out people already working in your target career or industry, and 4) Consider general skills necessary across almost all industries and careers.

Tip #1: Analyze the job requirements. First, carefully review requirements for the positions of interest in the new industry. What knowledge and skills are required? What experience is required? What type and level of education is required or preferred? Once you fully understand this information you'll be in a better position to analyze yourself and determine which skills are transferable.

Tip #2: Analyze yourself against the job requirements. An analysis of the job's requirements will be especially important when you're striving to change careers. Ask yourself which of the job requirements you fully meet, partially meet, or don't meet at all – use the Job Requirements Analysis document in the Appendix to help you do this. Think about the requirements you fully meet and brainstorm how you've used those required skills in the past so you can provide concrete examples. This will help demonstrate that your skills are transferable. For example, if the job in the new industry requires leading cross-functional teams, think through a few instances you could share with a hiring manager where you've successfully led cross-functional teams. Use the S.T.A.R. method we discuss in Chapter 17 to effectively share your experience.

For each job requirement you don't meet (or partially meet), brainstorm how you could gain the required knowledge, skills, experience, or education. Could you read books on the topic? Could you learn it on the job? Could you take an online or in-person class or attend a seminar? Would you need to obtain a new certification? Determine a learning plan of action for every requirement you don't meet, and be prepared to share this with the hiring manager.

Tip #3: Seek out people already working in your target career or industry. It is helpful to obtain feedback and insight from experts already working in your desired career or field of interest. So use your savvy networking skills to meet with people (offer to buy coffee or lunch) to discuss the job requirements and your self-assessment. Obtain the insider's opinion as to what he or she believes are the most important job skills to be successful in the position.

When you meet with the person, review your skills, experience, education, and accomplishments and ask for their feedback on which of your skills they see as the most transferable. After that, ask the insider if they see any areas of concern with your goal of changing careers or industries. Whatever issues the expert brings up about your background will most likely also be brought up by a hiring manager.

Tip #4: Consider general skills necessary across almost all industries and careers. There are also several skills that I believe are transferable, no matter the job or industry. These skills include critical thinking, collaboration, creativity, and communication.

- *Critical thinking:* This allows you to think through situations and solve problems, make decisions, and take appropriate action.
- *Collaboration:* This means you can effectively work with others (even those with opposing points of view) and build diverse teams.
- *Creativity:* This isn't just about being innovative, but being able to see what is not there or what needs to change – then making it happen.
- *Communication:* This is the ability to synthesize situations and data and then convey ideas both verbally and in writing.

As you analyze your skills and the requirements for the new job, make sure you consider the four skills I've listed above. Then, think about ways you could also demonstrate these skills to a hiring manager through previous jobs you've held, and how you would use these skills in the new position if you were hired.

Yes, you really can successfully change careers or industries, but it requires a process of analysis, planning, and practicing how you'll communicate your "story" to a hiring manager.

HOW ASKING FOR CONSTRUCTIVE CRITICISM CAN CHANGE YOUR CAREER

Have you ever asked someone you trusted, respected, or admired for his or her feedback and constructive criticism? If not, do it now! While it can sometimes be a terrifying experience (when *isn't* asking for feedback terrifying?), it just might change your career and your life.

Many years ago, I managed a global integration project that, once completed, would yield several new high-level positions, one of which, I really wanted. During dinner after an integration meeting, I ended up seated next to the CEO of the division. By dessert, I had worked up the courage to tell him I was interested in "throwing my hat in the ring" for the marketing job when it became available – I asked if he thought I could do the job.

After scratching his chin for a while he replied with something I wasn't expecting: *"No, at this time, I don't think you'd be able to do that job."*

My heart felt like it sank all the way to my feet. After picking myself up emotionally off the floor, I said, *"Tell me about that. I'd like to understand why you feel that way."* I didn't become defensive. I didn't get angry. I merely sought to understand his reasoning behind the comment.

He told me there were three areas in which he didn't think I could do the job, and then explained each. I quickly realized his perception of me didn't accurately match my skills and experience in two of those areas (although he had a good point about the third item).

I asked him: *"If I can prove my expertise in the first two areas and show you a plan to become an expert in the third area over the next 12 months, would you support me then?"* Thankfully, his answer was yes.

Over the next year, I demonstrated my skills and expertise in the areas he had questioned. I also created a plan of action for the third area, reviewed it with him for his feedback, and then worked my way though every single item. When the position was created and posted, I applied for the job and went through the rigorous interview process. And guess what? I earned the job.

Without the CEO's feedback, it is doubtful I would have gotten the position because I wouldn't have known he didn't think I was qualified in a few areas. I also probably wouldn't have learned this valuable lesson: My perception of myself might not always match the perception others hold of me, and the only way to find out is by asking for feedback. It was then that I realized perception (other people's perceptions, that is) often *does* equal reality.

Asking for constructive criticism can change your career and your life because, once you have the feedback, you can use it to improve yourself or work to change the perception of others. Here are some helpful hints for obtaining feedback:

- Begin by choosing people whose opinions you value.
- Speak with each person confidentially and explain what you're doing. Ask if they would be willing to meet with you to provide feedback.
- Respect someone's decision if they decide not to give it. Not everyone will be comfortable providing this kind of feedback. Schedule a mutually acceptable time and private location for the discussion. Be sure to choose a place where both of you are comfortable.
- Be prepared to ask him or her questions as well as follow up questions to any answers you don't understand.
- Don't get defensive. Listen to what they have to say even if their comments bruise your ego.
- Don't try to justify any past behavior. Remember, you are on an exploratory mission where you must choose not to take things personally or become offended.

Obtaining constructive criticism can be a powerful exercise. For some, it may confirm perceptions they already had of themselves. Others will find it to be an eye-opening experience and might be shocked at some of the feedback they receive. For the most part, you'll find that people feel flattered to be a part of your proactive career development.

Does obtaining feedback and constructive criticism really work? For me, it has provided an opportunity to learn things about myself that I didn't always know. The feedback also allowed me to adjust certain behaviors so I could positively impact the perception of others. What's not to love about that?

TEMPLATES

To assist you in completing the exercises, all templates are available electronically to download. Just go to the website, www.careerwomaninc.com and from the Home Page, click on "Resources" and then "Secrets from a Hiring Manager Turned Career Coach" – then scroll down and click on the "Templates" link and you may download the templates after you enter the password, **"Athena"**.

Personal Assesment

What adjectives would people who know me use to describe me?

_____

_____

What are my core values in life?

_____

_____

What is my definition of success?

_____

_____

What am I good at accomplishing at work?

_____

_____

_____

_____

_____

_____

What tasks do I dislike at work?

_____

_____

What do I want to be known for?

_____

_____

Future Job Assesment

What would be the description of my "perfect job"?

_____

_____

_____

_____

_____

_____

With what kind of people would I be working?

_____

_____

What kind of work would I be doing?

_____

_____

How would my work benefit me?

_____

_____

How would my work benefit the company or other people?

_____

_____

How would my work make me feel?

_____

_____

Aspiration Development

Things that are important to me in life:

_____

_____

_____

_____

Work things I'm good at:

_____

_____

_____

_____

Work things I don't enjoy:

_____

_____

_____

_____

My aspiration(s):

_____

_____

_____

_____

_____

Action Item Definition

ACTION	DESCRIPTION	TIMING

Company Research Information

Name of Company _____ Website URL _____

Office(s) Location(s) _____

Telephone # _____ # of Employees _____

Type of Company _____ Company Age _____

Total Annual Revenue _____ Revenue Growth % _____

Company History _____

_____

Products/Services _____

_____

Target Market _____

Characteristics of Typical Customer _____

_____

Key Competitors _____

Company Culture, Diversity, and Environment _____

_____

Recent News/Press Release Information _____

_____

Community Involvement _____

_____

Stated Business Goals _____

_____

Job Requirement Analysis

Company:_____ Position: _____

JOB REQUIREMENTS	MY ANALYSIS

S.W.O.T. Analysis

STRENGTHS	WEAKNESSES

OPPORTUNITIES	THREATS

Resume Example 1

Jane Doe 1

111 Washington Street, #A1, Anytown, ST 10001
Jane.Doe@JaneDoe.com | (111) 111-1111

EDUCATION

June 2008	**ABC UNIVERSITY**	City, ST

Master of Arts Degree, Communications
- GPA: 3.7

June 2006	**ABC UNIVERSITY**	City, ST

Bachelor of Arts Degree, Marketing Communications
- GPA: 3.5

EXPERIENCE

Summer 2008	**ACME, INC.**	City, ST

Public Relations Intern
- Created press releases and wrote speeches for the CEO

Summer 2007	**BETA CORP.**	City, ST

Marketing Communications Intern
- Re-created company website and produced marketing collateral for three new product launches

6/06-9/06	**CITY ZOO**	City, ST

Web Designer
- Created new interactive website - achieved increase in summer hit rates by just over 300%
- Achieved 99% customer satisfaction score from online zoo users

Summer 2005	**SELL MORE SOON, INC.**	City, ST

Web Design Intern
- Built new web pages for internal and external website
- Developed new online store functionality, resulting in online sales of $6 million within first six months after launch

6/00-6/05	**BEST RETAIL STORE**	City, ST

Sales Associate
- Worked full-time during every school vacation selling women's career clothing
- Earned "Pinnacle" award twice for achieving over 150% of sales quota
- Recognized three times for customer satisfaction award for going above and beyond the call of duty to help customers

SKILLS AND ACTIVITIES

Computer skills: Microsoft Office (Word, Excel, PowerPoint), Adobe Dreamweaver, NetObjects Fusion, HTML Editor, Javascript and Ajax

Volunteer work: Susan G. Komen Race for the Cure (website design and fundraiser), ABC University Career Fair (created communications plan, wrote press releases and provided on-site management coordination)

Resume Example 2

Jane Doe 2

222 Washington Street, #A1, Anytown, ST 22222
Jane.Doe@JaneDoe.com | (222) 222-2222

EXPERIENCE

4/05-4/09	**ALPHA CORP.**	City, ST

Supervisor, Customer Care Center
- Manage 50+ employees in 24x7 call center
- Restructured department including: Processes and policies, communications, and performance trending and analysis reporting for individuals and the department – doubling department productivity within one year
- Led a process improvement project which resulted in decreasing order processing time by 52% and increasing order accuracy to an all-time record of 98.2%
- Earned Green Belt Certification in Process Improvement through company-sponsored training program

8/02-4/05	**ALPHA CORP.**	City, ST

Order Processor, Customer Care Center
- Managed the processing and tracking of customer orders for four company divisions, sub-specializing in two other areas in order to provide back-up during times of high volume
- Provided order processing software training to all new department employees
- Received department awards for processing the highest number of customer orders during fiscal years 2003 and 2004

2/00-8/02	**ALPHA CORP.**	City, ST

Customer Service Representative, Customer Care Center
- Provided first line call center assistance for in-coming customer calls
- Uncovered bug in IT system, worked with software technicians to locate the problem, tested solutions prior to implementing IT fix
- Earned 2001 customer satisfaction award for outstanding customer service efforts

EDUCATION & MANAGEMENT DEVELOPMENT

Sept 2007	**ALPHA CORP.**	City, ST

Green Belt Certification in Process Improvement

Nov 2006	**BE A LEADER NOW**	City, ST

Leadership Training, 3-day course

May 2004	**AJAX TRAINING**	City, ST

Finance for the Non-Financial Manager, 2-day course

June 2000	**ABC UNIVERSITY**	City, ST

Bachelor of Science Degree, Business
- GPA: 3.3

ASSOCIATION MEMBERSHIP & ACTIVITIES

National Association of Female Executives (NAFE), Chamber of Commerce Women's Network, Alpha Corp Women's Mentoring Program, and volunteer mentor for Big Brother /Big Sisters Mentoring Program

Resume Example 3

Jane Doe 3

333 Washington Street, #A1, Anytown, ST 33333
Jane.Doe@JaneDoe.com | (333) 333-3333

SKILLS SUMMARY

- Call Center Management
- Performance Analysis & Trending
- Process Improvement
- Software Training
- Order Processing
- People Management

EXPERIENCE

4/05-4/09	**ALPHA CORP.**	City, ST

Supervisor, Customer Care Center
- Manage 50+ employees in 24x7 call center
- Restructured department including: Processes and policies, communications, and performance trending and analysis reporting for individuals and the department – doubling department productivity within one year
- Led a process improvement project which resulted in decreasing order processing time by 52% and increasing order accuracy to an all-time record of 98.2%
- Earned Green Belt Certification in Process Improvement through company-sponsored training program

8/02-4/05	**ALPHA CORP.**	City, ST

Order Processor, Customer Care Center
- Managed the processing and tracking of customer orders for four company divisions, sub-specializing in two other areas in order to provide back-up during times of high volume
- Provided order processing software training to all new department employees
- Received department awards for processing the highest number of customer orders during fiscal years 2003 and 2004

2/00-8/02	**ALPHA CORP.**	City, ST

Customer Service Representative, Customer Care Center
- Provided first line call center assistance for in-coming customer calls
- Uncovered bug in IT system, worked with software technicians to locate the problem, tested solutions prior to implementing IT fix
- Earned 2001 customer satisfaction award for outstanding customer service efforts

EDUCATION & MANAGEMENT DEVELOPMENT

Sept 2007	**ALPHA CORP.**	City, ST

Green Belt Certification in Process Improvement

Nov 2006	**BE A LEADER NOW**	City, ST

Leadership Training, 3-day course

May 2004	**AJAX TRAINING**	City, ST

Finance for the Non-Financial Manager, 2-day course

June 2000	**ABC UNIVERSITY**	City, ST

Bachelor of Science Degree, Business
- GPA: 3.3

Resume Tips

As you go about creating or updating your resume, here are tips to think about before you apply online:

- Choose an easy-to-read font, preferably a sans serif style such as Arial or Calibri.
- Use only one or two font styles within your resume.
- Ensure the font size is large enough to read (10-12 point).
- Resist the urge to cram in lots of information by shrinking the font size.
- Use bullets to itemize key accomplishments and quantify results, where possible.
- Use action verbs to describe your achievements, such as: created, implemented, improved, designed, directed, documented, organized, reduced, eliminated, negotiated, optimized, increased, achieved, accomplished, trained, resolved, etc.
- If possible, avoid words like: assisted, helped, and supported.
- Be concise and don't use long sentences.
- Don't use acronyms. Always spell out acronyms.
- Never use your existing work telephone number or work address. in your contact information. Preferably, use a personal mobile. telephone number and your home address (or leave your address off the document).
- Explain any significant gaps in work history, such as taking time out to raise children or to care for elderly parents.
- In the "Education" section, don't forget to include any relevant continuing education programs you've completed or certifications you've earned. And, if you have computer training or skills, be sure to list this if it's applicable to the job.
- Include your name and page number on each page (in case your resume pages get separated).
- Avoid using graphics, tables, horizontal lines, or hyperlinks because many electronic applicant tracking systems cannot read these.
- Include all important information in the body of the document, not in the header/footer function.

Resume Tips continued

- If you're just beginning your career, try to limit your resume to one page.
- If you've been in your career for many years, you don't need to limit your resume to one page – but don't write a novel. A resume should include only enough pertinent information to "hook" the reader to take further action.
- Customize your resume for each job for which you apply, and be sure you've included all pertinent key words.
- Create a resume that is simply formatted for electronic uploading, and save your creativity for the hardcopy resume you bring with you to the job interview.
- Save your resume into a PDF format before submitting online or emailing.
- DO NOT include personal information on your resume such as your age, race, religion, gender expression or identity, national origin, marital status, sexual orientation, veteran or military status, or physical, mental, or sensory disabilities. These are "protected classes" under most state laws (in the United States).
- Title your electronic resume appropriately using your name, the job title, company, and date you apply (using the international date format). Example: Jane Doe Resume_MarCom Mgr_Acme, Inc_15Sept2014

Reference List Example

Jane Doe

333 Washington Street, #A1, Anytown, ST 33333
Jane.Doe@JaneDoe.com | (333) 333-3333

REFERENCE LIST

John Smith
Title: Director, Customer Care Center
Company: ALPHA CORP.
Mailing Address: 1212 Any Street, Anytown, ST 22222
Email Address: John.Smith@ALPHACORP.com
Telephone: 222-111-1212
Relationship: Direct manager from 4/05 to 4/09; colleague for five years prior

Janice Jones
Title: Manager, Customer Care Center
Company: ALPHA CORP.
Mailing Address: 1212 Any Street, Anytown, ST 22222
Email Address: Janice.Jones@ALPHACORP.com
Telephone: 222-111-1313
Relationship: Direct manager from 8/02 – 4/05

Cheryl Adams
Title: Human Resources Manager, led internal women's mentoring program
Company: ALPHA CORP.
Mailing Address: 1212 Any Street, Anytown, ST 22222
Email Address: John.Smith@ALPHACORP.com
Telephone: 222-111-1414
Relationship: Cheryl leads the women's mentoring program, for which I am a volunteer mentor helping 3 other women

Tim Lee
Title: Director of Volunteers
Company: Big Brother / Big Sister Program
Mailing Address: 555 5th Avenue, Any Street, Anytown, ST 22223
Email Address: Tim.Lee@bigbrotherbigsister.org
Telephone: 222-333-2121
Relationship: I report to Tim for all volunteer activities, assignment of "little sisters," and progress reviews

Recommendation Letter 1

ALPHA CORP.

1212 Any Street, Anytown, ST 22222

April 2, 2009

To whom it may concern:

Please accept this letter of recommendation for Carol Roberts. I am the Director of the Customer Care Center for ALPHA CORP. I have known Carol for nine years, the past four years of which she reported directly to me, and she has been an absolutely outstanding employee. Due to the recent downsizing at the company, we were forced to "de-layer" and laid off 30% of our workforce, mainly middle-managers. While Carol was unfortunately one of those who had to be let go, I would hire her back in a heartbeat if I were given the opportunity.

Carol is highly skilled and experienced in all areas of business call centers. She began her career at ALPHA CORP. as a Customer Service representative and quickly distinguished herself by answering more customer calls and resolving more customer issues than any other representative in the company. When she was promoted into the area of order processing, we discovered her incredible knack for learning computer systems, training others on how to use the software, and even uncovering IT bugs. She also became the "go to" person within the department when it came to training all new hires. She is known for her patience and understanding when helping those with less computer and technology knowledge.

Carol actively seeks to continue improving herself and her skills year after year and while working as a Supervisor in the Customer Care Center, earned her Green Belt Certification in Process Improvement. She then led a project that resulted in significant results – she decreased our order processing time by 52% while at the same time achieved the highest order accuracy success rate in the history of the company, 98.2%. She also realized a need to restructure the department, created a recommendation plan that was approved, and then implemented the plan - and doubled productivity in the department within one year.

The day I was told I had to let Carol go from our company was one of the hardest days of my career. Carol was a tremendous asset to our company and to our department and I know she would be a tremendous asset to any company willing to use her talents. On a personal note, I believe you will find Carol to be friendly, dependable, and honest. These qualities have served her well in her previous positions and will continue to be assets to her throughout her career.

Please feel free to contact me if you have any questions or would like me to elaborate on any of my remarks. I cannot be more enthusiastic in providing Carol with my highest recommendation.

Sincerely,

John Smith

John Smith
Director, Customer Care Center
Email: John.Smith@ALPHACORP.com
Telephone: 222-111-1212

Recommendation Letter 2

ALPHA CORP.

1212 Any Street, Anytown, ST 22222

April 3, 2009

To whom it may concern:

I am writing this letter of recommendation for Carol Roberts. I am a Human Resources Manager for ALPHA CORP. and as the leader of the internal women's mentoring program I have had the pleasure of working with Carol for the last five years while she served as a volunteer mentor (in addition to her "normal" job at ALPHA).

During this time there were three key qualities I observed in Carol: 1) The ability to take difficult things and make them more easily understandable; 2) Excellent communication skills; and 3) Patience.

Carol is a very intelligent and catches on to things at a very fast pace. While people with this ability often find it difficult or irritating to work with slower paced individuals, Carol is quite the opposite – she is incredibly adept at taking difficult concepts and breaking them down in more manageable pieces then training others and helping them understand how things work.

Another key skill is her communication abilities. Carol provided me with support to pull together the overall mentoring program strategic plan and internal communication plan. She helped me create the foundation documents for the program as well as wrote all the verbiage we used to communicate the new program throughout the company, including: Emails, Intranet site page, posters, and speeches from our CEO.

Not only is Carol incredibly generous in giving up time to help others, but she also has the patience of a saint. It took a lot of work to get the women's mentoring program started at ALPHA CORP. and Carol was there to help, every step of the way. We look to her to mentor our most difficult employees because she always takes the time to understand their situation s and help them find positive alternatives to overcome barriers. She allows her mentees to discover the answers instead of merely telling them what to do.

Carol was let go from ALPHA CORP. due to downsizing only, not due to any performance issues. Her unfortunate departure has left a large hole in our mentoring program and she is missed tremendously. I highly recommend Carol for open positions within your company that fit her background – you will not be disappointed!

If you would like any further information, please do not hesitate to contact me.

Sincerely,

Cheryl Adams

Cheryl Adams
Manager, Human Resources
Email: Cheryl.Adams@ALPHACORP.com
Telephone: 222-111-1414

Recommendation Letter 3

Big Brothers / Big Sisters Program
555 5th Avenue, Anytown, ST 22223

April 3, 2009

To whom it may concern:

I am writing this letter of recommendation at the request of Carol Roberts. I am the Director of Volunteers for the Big Brothers / Big Sisters Program of Anytown. I first met Carol back in early 2002 when she applied to be a volunteer "big sister."

Over the last six years I have watched Carol help many young girls as well as other volunteers. Carol is incredibly gifted at listening to people, asking the right questions, and helping them determine ways to achieve their goals and dreams in life. In all my years of directing volunteer programs, I don't believe I've ever seen someone with as much passion, dedication, and ability to help others.

Everyone in the program looks toward Carol as a key leader - she leads by teaching and coaching others and by earning their respect over time. I believe all of the strengths Carol has displayed as a volunteer in our program could be well used in a business situation and I highly recommend Carol for consideration for a position within your company.

Should you wish for any additional information about Carol, please don't hesitate to give me a call or send me an email.

Sincerely,

Jim Lee

Tim Lee
Director of Volunteers
Telephone: 222-333-2121
Email: Tim.Lee@bigbrotherbigsister.org

Customized Cover Letter

Stephanie Smith

333 Washington Street, #A1, Anytown, ST 33333
Jane.Doe@JaneDoe.com | (333) 333-3333

April 6, 2009

XYZ Company
999 Right Way Road
Perfect City, WA 99999
Attn: Carrie Apple, Director, Sales Operations

Dear Ms. Apple:

Stacy Jones, Inside Sales Manager, suggested I contact you regarding the open position in the call center, Job ID #2727, Manager, Customer Center.

I have nine years experience working in a call center, the last four in a management position, with responsibilities including: hiring; training all new employees; supervising personnel; measuring and managing performance metrics; and, implementing several process improvement projects. I am highly experienced in ABC software platform, specifically; I helped create the internal user guides and training materials and then trained everyone when we migrated from the older software system to the ABC platform at my previous company.

My career passion has been working in call centers because of the internal and external customer interaction. I have experience in handling customer calls, working with internal and external sales representatives, processing orders, solving credit hold issues, and working with internal IT groups to resolve software bugs.

I am eager to speak with you about the employment opportunity at XYZ Company. I understand from Stacy that you will be attending the Chamber of Commerce networking event on Thursday evening. I am planning to participate in the event also and hope we have the opportunity to meet in person. If for some reason we don't connect on Thursday evening, I will plan to give you a call on Friday morning to schedule time for us to talk.

I've enclosed my resume for your consideration. If you wish to speak before Thursday evening, don't hesitate to give me a call.

Sincerely,

Stephanie Smith

Stephanie Smith

Interview Preparation Questions

Background Questions:

- Walk me through each job you've held and tell me the most important thing you learned in each position.
- Tell me about your most important career accomplishment.
- What is the toughest work challenge you've ever faced and how did you handle it?
- Tell me about your last few job performance appraisals. What were your evaluation results? What were you praised for and what were the suggestions for improvement areas?
- What have you done lately to "upgrade" yourself? (improve your knowledge or skills)
- What is your biggest failure to date?
- Why did you choose that college/university?
- Why did you choose that specific degree?
- What was your grade point?
- Do you believe grades are an indicator of how successful a person will be in their career? How so? Or, why?
- What classes/subjects did you enjoy the most when you were in school, and why?
- What classes/subjects did you enjoy the least when you were in school, and why?
- Did you work while you went to school? If yes, what did you do?
- How has your education prepared you for your career?
- When did you decide on this as your career?
- What made you decide on this as your career?
- What is your greatest strength?
- What is your biggest weakness?
- What is the toughest challenge you've ever faced and how did you face it?
- Why did you leave your last position?
- Why are you leaving your current job? Or, why did you leave your last job?
- What have you been doing since your last job?

Interview Preparation Questions

Job/Company/Industry Questions:

- Tell me what you know about this open position.
- What interests you about this job? Or, why do you want this job?
- Looking at the job description, take me through each requirement and explain why you believe you are qualified in each of the areas listed.
- Tell me what you know about this company and industry.
- Why do you want to work for this company?
- What do you believe it will take to be successful in this position?
- What interests you about our products or services?
- What criteria are you using to choose the companies to which you've applied?
- If you were the hiring manager for this position, what qualities would you look for to find the best candidate?
- Is there anything I haven't told you about the job, company, or industry that you'd like to know?

Functional Fit Questions (these will be specific to the job):

- *Sales job:* Walk me through the most complex sale you've ever made and why you believe it was complex. Explain each step in the sales process you typically follow.
- *Marketing job:* What are some of the biggest issues you've encountered in product launch plans, and, how did you overcome them? What are the components you typically include in a marketing plan?
- *Administrative assistant job:* What have you found are the most important skills for being successful in this type of role? Walk me through your skill level in preparing presentations. Tell me about the most difficult or complex presentation you ever created.
- *Database administrator job:* Walk me through your process of troubleshooting problems/issues.

Interview Preparation Questions

Style/Personality Questions:
- How would coworkers describe you?
- Tell me about your approach to setting goals for yourself.
- Describe your decision-making process.
- What do you believe is the best way to handle conflict?
- What frustrates you the most?
- Tell me about a situation where a conflict arose and you had to resolve it. What did you do?
- What motivates you?
- What is the best way to motivate a team?
- What is the best way to work on a team and be considered a team player?
- How would you handle a situation where you're working on a team project and one member is refusing to complete their work?
- How do you handle high-pressure situations?
- What is your definition of a leader?
- Tell me some specific examples of your leadership attributes.
- What qualities or attributes do you believe will contribute the most to your career success?
- Which do you believe is more important, being efficient or being creative?
- Would you rather work with people or information/data?
- Do you take work home with you?
- How many hours do you normally work each week?
- Tell me about a situation recently where you exceeded your manager's expectations.
- What's the best method to discipline an employee?
- How do you balance work with your personal life?
- What is the best compliment anyone has ever given you?
- What do people most often criticize about you?

Interview Preparation Questions

Future Orientation Questions:

- What are your career goals for the next five years? Ten years?
- Tell me about some of your recent career goals and what you've done to achieve them.
- How do you evaluate whether you or others have been successful?
- Tell me about some of the items on your personal development plan.
- Why should I hire you for this position over all the other candidates who have applied?
- If you could live your life over, what would you do differently?
- What have you learned from mistakes you've made in the past?
- Describe your work ethic.
- What is your definition of success?
- What do you believe are the key elements of measuring someone's performance?
- Are you willing to relocate?
- How willing are you to travel for work?
- Are you willing to work overtime?
- If I hired you, how long would you plan to remain with the company?
- What will you do if I don't hire you for this position?

Interview Preparation Questions

Cultural Fit Questions:

- Describe your ideal work environment.
- Explain a work environment or culture in which you would NOT be happy.
- Describe the behavior and characteristics of the best boss you've ever had.
- Tell me about your preferred work style (e.g. alone or on a team, with close supervision or allowed to work independently, fast-paced or slower paced).
- Explain your desired work environment or the environment in which you would be the most productive.
- Tell me about yourself.
- How would you describe yourself?
- What role are you most likely to play when working on a team? Provide an example.

S.T.A.R. Approach for answering, "Tell me about a situation when…" types of questions:

- **S** = Situation: Describe the situation
- **T** = Task: Explain the task or your main goal
- **A** = Action: Tell what actions you took
- **R** = Result: Highlight the positive results and try to quantify them, if at all possible

Questions to Ask the Hiring Manager

Questions about the hiring manager:

- How would you describe your leadership style?
- What are the reasons you decided to work for this company?
- What keeps you working here?
- What do you like the most and least about working here?

Questions about the position:

- Is this a newly created position or was there someone in it previously? If someone was in it previously, what did that person move on to do? (and are they still with the company?)
- What do you believe are the most important attributes necessary to be successful in this position?
- What do you think will be the most challenging aspects of the job?
- Can you explain the growth and advancement opportunities that will be available for this position?
- I always like to continue learning new things. Will there be opportunities for training and development?
- How would you describe a typical day or week in this position?
- How would you describe the best and worst aspects of this position?
- What do you see as my first priorities if I'm hired for the job?
- With whom will this position interact the most?
- How will my responsibilities and performance be measured? By whom? How often do performance appraisals occur?
- What do you see in my background, education, or skills that makes me attractive as a candidate for this position?

Questions to Ask the Hiring Manager

Questions about the department:

- How many people work in this department?
- What are the top priorities you're trying to accomplish in the department?
- What is the average tenure for department employees? Or, what is the turnover rate?
- When you think about trying to achieve your department objectives, what worries you or keeps you up at night?
- What is the reputation of the department within the company? (how are they perceived?)
- Could you explain the organizational structure to me? (for the department and the company)

Questions about the company:

- How would you describe the company culture? The company values?
- What do you see as the company's largest opportunities? Biggest threats?
- What are the company's short-term and long-term goals/objectives?
- How would you describe the management team's leadership philosophy at this company?
- What would you say are the skills and attributes of the most successful people at this company?
- How have the economic conditions affected the company?

Practice Interview Scoring Sheet

"Hiring Manager" Name: _____   "Interviewee" Name: _____

Date: _____

Style of "Hiring Manager":   □ Driver   □ Analytical   □ Expressive   □ Amiable

Entrance

□ Walks in exuding confidence   □ Shakes hand firmly   □ Smiles while shaking hands

Non-Verbal Interaction

□ Posture relaxed and confident   □ Positive eye contact   □ Relaxed facial expressions
□ Avoids distracting hand gestures   □ Does not fidget   □ Takes notes effectively

Rapport

□ Matches hiring manager's pace   □ Listens to understand   □ Asks clarifying questions
□ Accommodates style   □ Doesn't interrupt   □ Monitors defensiveness
□ Doesn't talk too much   □ Matches body language

Discussion

□ Confirms job requirements   □ Provides concise answers   □ Uses STAR approach effectively
□ Avoids "fluff" phrases   □ Summarizes major points   □ Explains their key differentiators
□ Uses "pause" technique effectively   □ Flows discussion smoothly   □ Recognizes objections or issues
□ Demonstrates knowledge of company
□ Asks appropriate questions of the interviewer

Closing

□ Recognizes closing signals   □ Advances "the sale"   □ Uses appropriate closing questions
□ Gains commitment to next steps   □ Knows when to leave   □ Thanks interviewer for their time

What they did well:

_____

_____

Areas for improvement:

_____

_____

Interview Attire

Name: _____ Company for Interview: _____
Environment / Culture of Company: _____
Geographic Location: _____ Weather/Temperature: _____

Clothing

☐ Pant Suit: _____
☐ Skirt Suit: _____
☐ Slacks: _____
☐ Blouse: _____
☐ Coat/Jacket: _____
☐ Scarf/Gloves: _____
☐ Cleaned? _____ ☐ Pressed? _____

Shoes

☐ Heels: _____
☐ Flats: _____
☐ Cleaned? _____ ☐ Shined? _____

Jewelry

☐ Necklace: _____
☐ Earrings: _____
☐ Cleaned? _____ ☐ Shined? _____

Other Items

☐ Briefcase: _____
☐ Notepad: _____
☐ Pen: _____
☐ Glasses: _____
☐ Contacts: _____
☐ Other: _____

Interview Preparation Checklist

Name: _____ Company for Interview: _____

Date of Inteview: _____ Time of Interview: _____

Securing the Job Interview

☐ Determined the kind of job wanted
☐ Researched the job requirements
☐ Researched the company and industry
☐ Analyzed the job requirements against my skills, experience, and education
☐ Conducted personal S.W.O.T. analysis
☐ Prepared resume
☐ Able to address any resume gaps
☐ Polished LinkedIn profile
☐ Conducted personal branding
☐ Prepared list of references
☐ Prepared portfolio of work (optional)
☐ Obtained recommendations
☐ Polished LinkedIn profile
☐ Conducted personal branding
☐ Found help from "sponsors" and "internal coaches"
☐ Wrote customized cover letter
☐ Submitted information
☐ Using tracking log to stay organized

Interview Preparation

☐ Prepared list of potential interview questions and answers
☐ Prepared questions for employer
☐ Conducted practice interviews
☐ Prepared to answer the toughest interview questions
☐ Practiced interview "closing" techniques
☐ Conducted practice interviews with family and friends
☐ Prepared to watch hiring manager's nonverbal cues
☐ Prepared to interview the company and hiring manager
☐ Determined interview attire – ready to project appropriate image

Document Preparation

☐ Made copies of resume
☐ Made copies of letters of recommendation
☐ Paper and pens
☐ Social Security card (or number)
☐ Fact sheet
☐ Printed copy of job posting

☐ Made copies of reference list
☐ Portfolio of work
☐ Driver's license
☐ Passport
☐ Thank you cards purchased and ready to use after interview

Arrival Preparation

☐ Address and telephone number
☐ Driving directions
☐ Breath mints

☐ Contact name and title
☐ Determined travel time necessary
☐ Mobile telephone (turn OFF)

Interview Follow-Up Notes

Name: _____ Company for Interview: _____

Date of Interview: _____ Name of Hiring Manager: _____

Time of Interview: _____ Location of Interview: _____

Observations about the office: _____

_____

Observations about the people I met: _____

_____

Observations about the company culture: _____

_____

Questions hiring manager asked me: _____

_____

_____

_____

Any issues that came up during the discussion: _____

_____

Documents I provided during or after interview: _____

_____

Any additional information I was asked to provide?   □ No □ Yes _____

What went well: _____

_____

What could have gone better: _____

_____

Job Search Tracking Log

COMPANY	POSITION/TITLE	DATE APPLIED	INFORMATION SUBMITTED & HOW	NEXT STEPS

NOTES

Notes

Notes

Notes

Notes

Notes

GLOSSARY

Career Aspirations: The goals you set for yourself that you want to achieve in your career. Example: Become a manager, start my own business, finish my degree and become a graphic designer, etc.

Career Coach: A person who works with clients to help them achieve their career goals and aspirations, such as obtaining a job, changing careers, obtaining a promotion, learning new skills, overcoming obstacles, improving weaknesses, managing people, or preparing for executive level roles.

Constructive Criticism: The process of obtaining feedback from those you trust who will offer their opinions about your work, your strengths and weaknesses, and areas for improvement.

Counter Offer: An offer made by your manager when you turn in your resignation letter. An example of a counter offer is when your manager offers you a higher salary if you will remain in you current job, instead of going to work for another employer.

Cultural Fit Interview: The goal of a cultural fit interview is to assess the job candidate's personal and social/work styles and preferences to ensure the person is a good fit within the hiring organization's culture. HR reps/recruiters often conduct cultural fit interviews, but in small companies this responsibility may fall on the hiring manager.

Customized Cover Letter: A cover letter that accompanies your resume when you apply for a specific job. The letter is customized to that job by including an opening paragraph referencing the job and job ID# of the position you're seeking, how you found out about the position (if relevant) and/or the person who referred you. A middle paragraph or two that briefly explains why you believe you are the best person for the job. And, a closing paragraph that establishes the next steps for contact.

Differentiators: Just as products have strengths that set them apart, so do people. Differentiators are the things you do better than others. They are the knowledge, skills, or experience that will set you apart from other job candidates and that make you special.

Functional Fit Interview: These types of interviews are usually conducted by the hiring manager and include questions and tests that assess job candidates' knowledge, skills, and experience for a specific job. A functional fit interview might also include assessment tests to determine how well the candidate performs in required areas, such as coding skills for IT positions, writing and editing skills for public relations jobs, or typing skills for administrative assistants.

Hiring Manager: The person who is responsible for making the hiring decision for a specific job.

HR Recruiter: A person who works to fill job openings for a company. These individuals develop and implement local and national recruiting plans, work with hiring managers to develop job descriptions and job postings, seek job candidates, screen applicants, and coordinate job offers.

Internal Coach: Someone who works at your target company and provides you with the information you need, but maybe doesn't know you well enough to agree to recommend you or doesn't know the hiring manager well enough to speak to them about you (or just aren't comfortable doing so). Use an internal coach to guide you through the company hiring process and to help you avoid pitfalls.

Internal Sponsor: Someone who works at your target company, provides you with background information, and answers your questions. They will also step up and vouch for you and your abilities and speak with the hiring manager and the assigned HR recruiter on your behalf. Use an internal sponsor to proactively open doors to a job, introduce you to hiring managers, or to help with your career advancement.

Job Offer: A formal offer of employment, usually provided by the hiring manager or HR person. May be verbal or written, and includes the terms and conditions of the job, such as salary/pay, holidays, start date, and any other job requirements.

Job Requirements: These are found within a job posting, usually as a bulleted list. Download the job posting and carefully examine it *before* you apply for any positions. Analyze your knowledge, skills, experience, and education to see how you compare to the job requirements and to identify gaps. When you fully understand the requirements, you can position yourself as the best possible candidate.

LinkedIn: A social networking website designed for business professionals. It allows you to share work and career related information with other users, keep an online list of professional contacts, participate in work-related discussions, follow the activities of specific companies and people, and search for job opportunities.

List of References: A list of professional contacts, such as former managers, coworkers, direct reports, clients or customers, or vendors – people with whom you have had a business relationship. Potential employers verify your job qualifications, personal integrity, and ethics by contacting references. If you are just beginning your career and don't have professional references, you should include personal or character references, such as former college professors or high school teachers, past athletic coaches, leaders of community service organizations where you've been a volunteer, or long-time family friends and neighbors. Avoid using immediate family members (such as your mom, dad, sister, or brother) as personal references.

Nonverbal Communication: The aspects of communicating that do not involve verbal communication, such as body language and posture, gestures, facial expressions, eye movements, attire, space (proximity to another person), etc.

Personal Branding: Treating yourself as a product, and using the business technique of branding to market yourself within your company or industry. Used by job candidates and career changers to stand out to recruiters, hiring managers, higher-level management, and even industry experts or those looking for experts. If done correctly, personal branding can positively impact your career and job search efforts.

Personal "Time Out": To start finding your career passion, give yourself a personal "time out" from the chaos of life and the workplace by focusing on reflection and exploration. This includes considering what makes you happy, your core values in life, your definition of success, your work strengths and weaknesses, even the description of your perfect job. The goal of taking a personal "time out" is to clarify the type of job that would better fit your skills, values, and passions in life.

Portfolio of Work: A collection of examples of previous work that can be used to show to hiring managers to demonstrate the quality of your work and how your projects have benefited previous employers and clients. Not everyone needs a portfolio of work examples for job interviews, but it can be helpful if you work in a career field where you have created tangible items and/or achieved measurable results that display your skills and expertise.

Recommendation Letter: A letter written by someone who has had a business relationship with the job candidate. In the letter, the writer assesses the strengths, differentiators, behavior, and ability of the job candidate to perform the desired job.

Resume: A resume is a document that lists, very concisely, your job experience, skills, accomplishments, and education. Your resume is typically the first item a potential employer will see. This means it needs to be the best advertisement possible, selling you as the best candidate for the job.

Resume Gap: A length of time in which you were not employed. There may be many reasons for resume gaps, such as being laid off due to downsizing, lack of availability of jobs after high school or college, taking time out to raise children, caring for sick relatives or elderly parents, taking a sabbatical, taking time off to go back to school full-time, taking time off for medical reasons, etc.

S.T.A.R. Process: An approach to answering *"Tell me about..."* interview questions. Begin by describing the situation (S). Explain the task or your main goal (T). Tell what actions you took (A). End by highlighting the positive results you achieved (R) and try to quantify your results, if at all possible.

S.W.O.T. Analysis: A valuable process companies use to assess themselves and their competitors to formulate their strategies that can easily be applied to job seekers, career changers, and career ladder climbers. S.W.O.T. stands for strengths (S), weaknesses (W), opportunities (O), and threats (T). This analysis process is used to capture information about your internal strengths and weaknesses as well as external opportunities and threats.

Telephone Interview: Screening interviews conducted by HR personnel and hiring managers to assess cultural and functional fit prior to holding an in-person interview with the job candidate. This is an inexpensive and fast method to eliminate candidates who are not qualified or not a good fit for the open job. Always treat telephone interviews as seriously as in-person interviews.

Temporary Work Agencies: Temporary work agencies, also known as temp agencies or temp staffing firms, hire workers and then place them in assignments at other companies. Companies approach these temp agencies, define their worker needs, and then sign contracts for the agencies to supply the workers. These are usually full-time positions and can range from short-term, such as several weeks, to indefinite periods of time, such as six months and longer. Company placements can be in small start-ups all the way to multi-billion dollar global corporations. In the past, temp agencies were known for supplying lower-skilled workers for entry-level type jobs. Today, most temp agencies provide highly skilled workers in a wide variety of industries and within many different job categories, such as: accounting and finance, call center and customer service, hospitality, marketing and communications, creative/graphic design, engineering, industrial and manufacturing, information technology, project management, process improvement, science, medical, transportation and warehousing, office and administrative.

INDEX

I WANT TO HEAR FROM YOU

I want to hear how this book has changed, helped, or inspired you. *How have you applied the techniques in this book to your job search? How has it helped you obtain recruiter inquiries or get prepared for job interviews? Did this book help you get a job? If so, how?* Tell me about your experiences because I'd love to hear them.

Visit **www.careerwomaninc.com** and share your story and experience.

You can also share your comments on Facebook at: **www.facebook.com/careerwomaninc**

Send me a message on Twitter to: **@careerwomaninc**

Conect with me via LinkedIn at: **linkedin.com/in/lisaquast**

ABOUT THE AUTHOR

LISA QUAST

Former Fortune 500 executive vice president and general manager, currently a business consultant, organizational trainer, certified executive coach, and award-winning career development author and blogger.

During my career in business, I climbed to the highest rungs of the proverbial career ladder and succeeded in industries, jobs, and at companies that were traditionally male-dominated. And I loved every minute of it (well, almost every minute). I made it my personal goal to learn about and work in as many different areas of business as possible, so I could fill my head and my heart with knowledge about how companies run and how people worked together.

In an interesting twist, I was often approached by women and asked to be their career mentor or to help them obtain their dream job. HR personnel also frequently asked me to mentor both women and men within the companies at which I worked. And I loved every minute of it (that part, I really did)!

What probably surprised people the most was that I've never believed in razzle-dazzle outlandish actions when it comes to work or career advancement. For me, it has always been more important to understand business fundamentals and to break complex situations down into the smallest, manageable parts.

Now you know my secret – *it is all about going back to the basics and being great at the fundamentals,* while bringing compassion and a childlike curiosity into everything I do. I hope you enjoy the book and find it helpful!

Please connect with me at www.careerwomaninc.com, on Facebook at **facebook.com/careerwomaninc**, on Twitter **@careerwomaninc**, or via LinkedIn at **linkedin.com/in/lisaquast**